Pacific Rim Park

A Country Doctor's Role in Preserving Long Beach and Establishing the New Wickaninnish Inn

Howard McDiarmid

Library and Archives Canada Cataloguing in Publication

McDiarmid, Howard, 1927-

      Pacific Rim Park : a country doctor's role in preserving Long Beach and establishing the new Wickaninnish Inn / Howard McDiarmid.

ISBN 978-0-9813204-0-3

      1. McDiarmid, Howard, 1927–. 2. Pacific Rim National Park Reserve (B.C.)—History. 3. Physicians—British Columbia—Tofino Region—Biography. 4. Legislators—British Columbia—Biography. 5. Wickaninnish Inn—History. 6. Tofino (B.C.)—Biography. 7. Ucluelet (B.C.)—Biography. I. Title.

FC3849.T65Z49 2009   971.1'203092   C2009-904307-6

Published by Howard McDiarmid, Victoria, BC

Available from   Wickaninnish Inn
                  Box 250
                  Tofino, BC V0R 2Z0
                  www.wickinn.com/

Cover and interior design: Jim Bisakowski, Desktop Publishing Ltd.
Editing: Audrey McClellan
Front cover photo of Wickaninnish Inn: Adrian Dorst, courtesy of the Wickaninnish Inn
Back cover photo of Peter Devries and the Shell Beach cabin: Jeremy Koreski

Printed and bound in Canada

14 13 12 11 10 09 1 2 3 4 5 6

To my lovely wife, Lynn, who married me for better or for worse, but not for politics, who nonetheless persevered through two elections and six years as a politician's wife with loyalty and understanding, sustained always by a wry sense of humour.

Contents

Acknowledgements

I would like to thank the staff of the BC Legislative Library, who produced copious quantities of old but pertinent newspaper articles and long-forgotten speeches.

Thank you to Kari-Anne Caswell, who translated almost illegible "doctor's writing" through many hours of typing.

Thanks to Audrey McClellan, who unequivocally demonstrated the necessity of having a great editor.

A special thanks to Grace McCarthy for writing a gracious foreword and postscript, and for her tireless work as an MLA and cabinet minister, promoting Beautiful British Columbia over many years.

Thanks to photographers Adrian Dorst and Jeremy Koreski for the stunning images on the front and back covers.

Thank you to my wife, Lynn, without whose faith, sacrifice and encouragement the inn would never have been built. And thank you to my three sons, Charles, Jim and Bruce, who campaigned for their dad and did hard physical work on the property to greatly enhance its value.

I would especially like to thank my son Charles McDiarmid, manager of the Wick Inn, who early on became a believer in my vision and prepared himself by graduating in hotel administration from Cornell University and gaining invaluable experience with the Four Seasons Hotel Group. He has become a consummate hotelier, with many awards to his credit, and has made us all proud of the Inn.

Foreword

The creation of Pacific Rim National Park Reserve is the story of one man's dream to conserve one of Canada's national treasures on the Pacific in the province of British Columbia.

This book recalls the contributions of some who had a part in ensuring that unbridled development and ad hoc plans would not rob future generations of this unrivalled place of wonder, serenity and beauty.

The Dreamer

However, it was the dream of Dr. Howie McDiarmid that inspired the Vancouver Island communities to get behind the vision for a national park. It was his tenacity and commitment to the dream that led him to run for public office. In the book, Howie explains the skill of former premier W.A.C. Bennett, who, the reader will learn for probably the first time, was, with Howie's persistence, instrumental in concluding a successful negotiation to establish the park.

The Doctor

This book is also about early days in British Columbia and exposes the very human side of a doctor with limited resources, working in uncharted waters in small, isolated BC communities with transportation challenges. It emphasizes the sacrifices of these early doctors and nurses who have helped to build the modern medical model we have today.

Dr. Howie McDiarmid has written a wonderfully entertaining commentary on parties (the social kind), politics and people.

Howie, you've made a difference in the lives of British Columbians! Well done!

Grace McCarthy, OC, OBC
Vancouver, April 2009

One

Welcome to Tofino

I stood on the tarmac at the Tofino airport on an overcast, grey, drizzly day in early January 1955 and watched the Queen Charlotte Airlines Canso flying boat disappear through the clouds back to Vancouver. There I was, for better or for worse, the only doctor in the remote village of Tofino. I wondered who should be more fearful, me or the townspeople, my future patients.

I came to be here as a result of a message posted on the interns' message board at Vancouver General Hospital where, in June 1954, I was nearing the end of a one-year rotating internship. I had previously finished four years' study and graduated in medicine from the University of Manitoba, but I needed a year of internship to be granted an MD. I hated cold winters, having grown up on the prairies in Prince Albert, Saskatoon, Calgary and Edmonton, so the milder weather of Vancouver and the West Coast was appealing, and I secured an internship at Vancouver General Hospital. I was fortunate to get this posting as my academic record was very average. My one remaining tie to Winnipeg was a student nurse, Lynn Honeyman.

As the internship year was coming to an end, I still had no idea what I wanted to do when it was over. Then one day a note appeared on the interns' bulletin board. A group of Catholic nuns wanted to reopen a hospital near Zeballos, a once-thriving gold-mining centre on the west coast of Vancouver Island, and needed the services of a physician to make their project feasible. They offered to pay the airfare for a doctor who would visit Zeballos to assess the situation. What did I have to lose?

Reservations were made, and I boarded the Canso at the Vancouver airport. We flew to Tofino, where we landed on an old World War II airstrip, and then on to Tahsis, where we landed in the middle of the bay. Needless to say, Cansos were amphibian.

The community of Tahsis was an evolving logging and sawmill site, population about 2,000, founded in 1945 by the entrepreneurial Gibson brothers, who were both politically active Liberals. In 1952 the Gibsons' company, which included the town, was purchased by a Danish conglomerate, the East Asiatic Company.

I was met by executives of the mill and an RCMP corporal who took us to the hospital site, about 20 miles toward Zeballos by boat. Neither Zeballos nor Tahsis was accessible by road at that time.

We visited the old hospital, but by that time I realized that trying to service the centre of population in Tahsis from a hospital 20 miles away by boat would be a logistical nightmare.

I reboarded the Canso and it took off from Tahsis, making another stopover on the runway at the Tofino airport where, to my surprise, I was met by a delegation of three members of the Tofino hospital board. They had learned of my trip to Tahsis via the West Coast Moccasin Telegraph. Chairman Tom Gibson and board members Doug Busswood and Bert Demeria set about to tell me why I should come to Tofino. As I had already made up my mind not to go to Tahsis, it didn't take much to convince me to take the Tofino job.

I learned that the previous Tofino Hospital had burned down, and there had been a vicious fight between Tofino and Ucluelet, two communities separated by 25 miles of bad road, as to where the new hospital would be located. At that time the population of Tofino was about 400, Ucluelet about 800, and the Native population more than the two combined. As a result, even though it was the smaller community, Tofino won the contest because of its proximity to the Ahousat, Opitsat and Hot Springs Cove Indian reserves, and the hospital was rebuilt there. Fortunately I didn't have a horse in that race, so I was able to play a peacekeeping role once I arrived on the coast.

I was unprepared to go to a solo remote practice that was only accessible by boat or plane, and then only when the weather was good, so I spent the next four months at Vancouver General Hospital learning as much about anesthetics and emergency surgery as possible. (One of the anesthetists who was particularly helpful was Lois Crawford. Coincidentally, her husband, Jeff Crawford, would later partner with Robin Fells to build the original Wickaninnish Inn on Long Beach, near Tofino.) I purchased two books, *Atlas of Surgical Operations* and *Early Diagnosis of the Acute Abdomen*, that became my bibles.

In spite of this preparation, I felt a great deal of apprehension as I watched the Canso leave after dropping me off at Tofino in January 1955. A car arrived and delivered me to the home of Walter and Clara Arnet, long-time Tofino residents. I was installed in an upstairs bedroom, but the only phone was downstairs, which meant Walter and Clara were awakened by every nighttime emergency call. They did not complain, but it was obviously a situation that could not last.

The Tofino hospital board gave me a small office and examining room in the hospital, and similar accommodation was provided in Ucluelet. The hospital was well-equipped, with 17 beds, four bassinettes and a pediatric ward of ten cribs. We had a surgical operating room and an obstetrical delivery room. There was a McKesson anesthetic machine that, while not that modern, delivered nitrous oxide and oxygen in proportion, controlled by one dial, which made it next to foolproof. We had an x-ray machine and an excellent radiographer, Ruby Arnet. The hospital staff were competent and caring, headed by Myrt Dickenson, who also assisted with anesthetics.

I saw patients in Tofino on Monday, Wednesday and Friday and in Ucluelet on Tuesday and Thursday. My father had presented me with a car upon my graduation, as much for relief at my graduation as a reward. It was a powder-blue Chevy Bel Air that had to put up with the abuse of the washboard road between Tofino and Ucluelet, rust from proximity to the ocean, and leaks from intense wind and rain. They didn't make cars as reliable in those days, so it became almost a routine to park the car with George Gudbranson at the garage in Ucluelet, go to the office, then retrieve the car at the end of the day. The car was so porous that a green mould grew in the back seat. I used to kid that I was growing my own penicillin.

My apprehension about my ability to cope gradually diminished as I found out my training enabled me to deal with the emergencies of a small, isolated practice better than I expected. Nonetheless, having no easy access to specialists was a concern, and in times of uncertainty there was no one to turn to but myself.

I immediately subscribed to numerous medical books and journals, particularly *Medical Clinics of North America*, *Pediatric Clinics of North America*, annual books of obstetrics and gynecology, along with the *Canadian Medical Journal* and *New England Journal of Medicine*, gradually building up a reference library.

Because I had interned at VGH, I knew who all the best specialists were and had great confidence in them. It was far better for me to refer patients to a competent specialist rather than have them seek a second opinion from someone of unknown capability. I particularly remember Don Munroe, a specialist in internal medicine, John Boyd in obstetrics, Henry Dunn in pediatrics, Jack McDougal in surgery and Howard Smith in urology.

Trying to contact them for advice over the phone was a challenge, though. The phone was of the old crank variety, and when we made a connection it often sounded like thunder or galloping horses were rumbling in the background, but it was better than no phone at all.

Shortly after arriving in Tofino, I was called in early one evening to see a woman who was diabetic and had stopped taking her insulin when her supply ran out. She was on the verge of diabetic coma, so I rushed her to hospital and ordered immediate treatment with fast-acting crystalline insulin. After about 20 minutes of frantic searching, I discovered that the hospital had inadvertently run out of insulin. There were no other known diabetics in the area. What to do? I was able to get in touch with Don Munroe, the best internist I knew in Vancouver, and he advised giving certain intravenous solutions we had on hand to ameliorate the acid condition in her blood. At the same time, I chartered a plane to arrive at first light with the lifesaving insulin. The woman survived.

The more I got to know people in the community, the more I liked them. There was no class distinction between the hard-working loggers, fishermen and miners, who worked in dangerous occupations and were no-bullshit people, and the healthy dollop of intellectual iconoclasts who hated cities and marched to their own drummers. Tofino then, in marked contrast to now, was very much a live and let live community.

I became particularly friendly with Bill and Ruth White. Bill was a raconteur without peer and the funniest man I had ever met. Ruth shared her husband's delight in a good story well told. Bill ran the local crab cannery with his partner, Pierre Malon. Bill did most of the crabbing while Pierre looked after the cannery. Together they produced a high-quality product that was in great demand.

When it came time to replace his original crab boat, *Belle*, Bill found it was cheaper to have the new vessel built in Nova Scotia and shipped by rail to Vancouver than to have it built in Vancouver. He had an impish sense of humour and loved to put one over on the establishment. The federal Department of Transport had to approve the names of all boats, looking carefully for double meanings—although it wasn't too stringent. I know of one sailboat that was called *Passing Wind*. Bill thought he could get away with calling his new crab boat "Blue Ointment," which during World War II was the favoured treatment for the condition Pediculosis pubis, also known as crab lice or, even less politely, as crotch crickets. Before Bill could send in his application with that name, saner heads prevailed and it was called *Stubbs Isle*.

My wife, Lynn, with Ruth and Bill White, who became very close friends during my early years in Tofino.

Stubbs Island, known to the locals as Clayoquot (pronounced *Kla-qwot*), is the island just off Tofino and was the site of the first licensed premises in the area. When I arrived, the pub was run by Bill White's two sisters, the formidable Betty Farmer and Jo Bridges, but during World War II, Bill and Ruth had managed it. He told me of one Labour Day weekend when the miners were busy, the loggers were cutting spruce for Mosquito bombers, and there was a huge crew building the three 5,000-foot runways and two huge hangars that would become the Tofino airport. The workers had all downed tools for the long weekend and headed for Clayoquot, quickly overwhelming the tiny beer parlour. The party flowed out to the adjacent lawns and boats at the dock, continuing through Saturday, Sunday and into Monday, at which point the RCMP patrol boat arrived at the dock. Corporal Green started making his way up the path to the hotel. Bill came down to meet him and the corporal told him, "All right, Bill, shut her down." To which Bill replied, "No, you shut her down. You've got the gun."

The people of Tofino still knew how to party when I was there. I had been working hard for four months, on call 24 hours a day, when the Tofino Hospital nurses put on a dance at the air force base, which after the war had become a radar site. There were about 100 air force personnel at the base, and they had a small medical office in which I saw routine cases once a week. I was also an honorary member of the officers' mess. I was invited to the dance and was having a great time when, about ten o'clock, a call came from the hospital. A woman from Ahousat had just arrived by boat in advanced labour, and I had best get there post-haste.

By the time I arrived, she was already in the delivery room and in stirrups. I quickly scrubbed and gowned and examined her, ascertaining that she was close to delivery. At this point her contractions virtually ceased and all progress ground to a halt. As medical students, we were all taught that the treatment for this condition, called uterine inertia, was tincture of time: Do nothing until things start up again on their own. I kept thinking of the party slipping by and was pacing the delivery room in frustration.

Finally I said to the poor woman, "I wish you had this baby last night."

After a brief pause, and with baleful eyes, she looked up at me and said, "So do I."

This put everything in perspective, and I apologized to her for my insensitive remark. She delivered the baby three hours later. This incident helped me to think more in terms of the patient's point of view.

When I first arrived in Tofino, I had planned to stay maybe six months, enough time to build up a stake that would allow me to go and visit Europe. But as the six-month milestone approached, I realized I felt like I belonged here, and I wanted to stay. I liked the people and I liked the place.

Although winter in Tofino was never really cold, there were many grey days, sometimes lasting for weeks on end, which could be depressing. Then one day the sun would come out and reveal blinding beauty. The grey days were forgotten and all was forgiven. I didn't fully appreciate the beauty of the place until I visited some of the outer island beaches with Bill and Ruth in their tiny boat *Belle*, but what really opened my eyes was a flight down the coast from Tofino to Ucluelet. Beach after beach, bay after bay, some big, some small, some grandiose, like Long Beach, but all different. I have yet to see a more varied and picturesque 30 miles of coastline.

If I were going to stay, I would need a house. It just so happened that Chris Green, who worked with me at the hospital, had a brother, Gordon, who was leaving the area and had a small house for sale for $4,000. I bought it.

There was also that lone tie to Winnipeg in the form of Lynn Honeyman, who I mentioned earlier in the chapter. I had had several dates with Chris Green, who was a really nice woman, but thoughts of Lynn kept surfacing in my mind, and now I had to do something about them.

Two

Getting Hitched

We all have friends and experiences early in our lives that shape our later lives and actions significantly. This is certainly true in my experience. When I was growing up, my father was a manager with the Imperial Bank of Canada (which later merged with the Bank of Commerce to become the CIBC). This meant we moved around the prairie provinces a lot, and one such move, to Prince Albert, Saskatchewan, occurred just before I started Grade 1.

It was not a happy time. I was the new kid on the block, and because of my protruding ears the other kids dubbed me Mickey Mouse and routinely taunted and harassed me, chasing me home from school at the end of the day. I was miserable.

This all changed when the Harradence family moved in next door. Clyne was two years older than I was, and Milt was four years older, and they became my protectors. Our parents subsequently built cottages at Emma Lake, where we swam, boated and played tennis together. These were idyllic times, and I learned to love the warmth of summer.

My old friend Milt Harradence (right) in 2003, along with Jimmy Miles.

Just as I finished Grade 8, however, my father received a promotion and we moved to Saskatoon for a year. Another promotion took us to Calgary, where the winters were still cold but, with the miraculous chinook winds occurring every so often, not as cold as Prince Albert or Saskatoon.

One night my dad took me to the Calgary armoury to see a boxing card featuring Armed Forces personnel. Who should be boxing but Milt Harradence. He was a fine athlete and a good boxer. We brought him back to our house for a home-cooked dinner, and I subsequently took him to the Glencoe Club for tennis, where he met his future wife, Cal Richardson. The war ended soon after that, and Milt and Clyne entered law school at the University of Saskatchewan in Saskatoon.

In Grade 12, the decision of what to do with my life began to loom. I wanted to do something that would put the choice of where to live in my hands, not leave it to the whim of a corporation, and the idea of being a doctor began to percolate in my mind. As a result, I enrolled in pre-med at the University of Alberta in Edmonton, earning a bachelor of science degree there before entering first-year medicine at the University of Manitoba in Winnipeg.

I was not wildly enthusiastic about the study of medicine. The workload was far heavier than I had imagined and much less interesting than expected. Summer breaks were a different story. Thanks to my father's contacts, I was able to secure a job as a bellhop at the Banff Springs Hotel in Alberta's Banff National Park. I met students from all across Canada and from all walks of life there, and the experience expanded my view of the world. Bellhops received good tips, and I was proud of the fact that I could take care of my university expenses until Christmas each year.

Bellhops at Banff Springs Hotel, ca. 1947. I am second from left in the front row.

My good friend and fraternity brother Russ Dixon worked in the same capacity at Lake Louise, and he introduced me to the fine art of fly fishing. Almost every other weekend we would plan a hike to a different lake, each reputed to be full of hungry trout. More often than not the lake did not live up to expectations for the number of fish caught, and we would lament, "She must be fished out!" We were never deterred from future hikes, though, and over time it dawned on me that it was the hike that was important. The experience of being surrounded by pristine mountains, forests and mountain meadows made me appreciate natural beauty and the importance of its preservation.

Early in my final year of medicine I was working in the pathology lab with another student, surrounded by the ugliest possible aberrant specimens, when I glanced up and saw the most attractive young woman in student nurse attire—an astounding contrast to what I had been looking at. I asked my classmate if he knew who she was. He didn't, but he thought he could find out.

A day or two later he had a name, "Pat Honeyman," and a phone number. I had never felt such a sudden attraction for someone and was determined to act, so I immediately phoned the number. The call was answered by a young woman. I said I was hoping to speak to a student nurse named Pat Honeyman. The woman at the end of the line replied that she was a student nurse, but her name was Lynn. Her sister, who was definitely not a student nurse, was named Pat.

We talked for a while, and I told her I was a medical student and had seen her in the lab. Medical students had the reputation of being somewhat crass, and I really wanted to impress her, so I asked her if she would come with me to a performance of the Winnipeg Ballet.

She was somewhat surprised but acquiesced. The date went well. Lynn wasn't sure what to make of me, but she did agree to another date. This led to another and yet another, and soon we were seeing only each other. That Christmas she presented me with a sweater she had knitted herself. My mother attached great significance to this.

We got along really well, and if it wasn't love, it was close, but neither of us were ready to talk of marriage. I was due to intern in Vancouver, and Lynn still had a year to go before receiving her degree. We had one sad final date before we went our separate ways. Now here I was, 18 months later, wondering if we might still get back together.

Lynn had graduated from Winnipeg General around the time I moved to Tofino, and together with her friend Edith Anderson, she had gone to nurse in Bermuda.

I wrote to her and, with the fear of rejection strong in my heart, allowed as how a friend of mine would be visiting Bermuda. Would she be available to show him around? It seemed to take weeks for her reply to arrive, but when it did she said she would be glad to do it. What a relief.

Next I had to get my friend Jimmy Miles to come and take over the practice temporarily—technically called a locum tenens or just plain locum. While in Tofino he stayed with my good friends Ruth and Bill White. They got along famously and became lifelong friends.

It was a very surprised Lynn who saw me get off the plane. We soon rediscovered that there was something special between us. She continued to work most days, but one afternoon we were sitting on a hill overlooking Hamilton Harbour, the blue ocean contrasting with pastel houses, sailboats bobbing in the wind, which prompted me to say, "Let me take you away from all this."

It took her two days to decide, but finally the answer was yes. We needed a special dispensation from the government to get a marriage licence. Lynn had to scrub on a surgical case that morning, but on the afternoon of June 24, 1955, we were married in St. Andrews Church.

The only way I could let my family know was via a collect call. When my dad picked up the phone and the operator said, "You have a collect call from your son in Bermuda. Will you accept the call?" he replied, "I don't have a son in Bermuda."

I quickly interjected, "Oh yes you do."

I then gave him the news, to which he replied, after a long pause, "I hope it was not just a matter of propinquity."

When I reassured him that Lynn was from Winnipeg and her father was a manager of the Canada Permanent Mortgage Corporation, there was much relief.

When we finally headed north to Canada, the last leg of our trip home was by de Havilland Beaver from Port Alberni to Ucluelet. It was overcast and rainy—what else is new?—and we flew 20 feet above the water, finally landing to dock at a float partially under water. Lynn was in summer clothes and high heels. If the plane had not turned and left so quickly, I think she might have gone with it.

We were met by Jimmy Miles and Ruth White, who fortuitously had a glass rolling pin filled with rye whisky. On the way to our little home, we stopped to visit Bill's cannery so we could introduce Lynn to the ten or so women sitting at a long cement table, picking shells out of the crab meat for the canning.

The previous owner had taken most of his furniture when he moved out of the house. We had a mattress on the floor, and the refrigerator was in the bedroom. The kitchen was too small to accommodate it. We did have two bottles of overproof rum and a handful of Bermuda swizzle sticks. What marriage could not survive a start such as this!

Three

Adventures in Medicine

Soon after Lynn arrived in Tofino, she took up duties at the hospital. Among her other tasks, she became my surgical nurse assistant. Late one night a pregnant woman from Ahousat arrived by boat, bleeding heavily from her vagina. It was her twelfth pregnancy, and she had not seen anyone for prenatal care. After careful physical and x-ray examination, we diagnosed her as having a complete placenta previa. In this condition, the placenta completely covers the cervix, the baby's exit route from the womb. Without intervention in the form of a caesarean section, this condition will cause the death of mother and child.

I had never done a c-section before, although I had assisted in a few. Nonetheless, there was no option. This could not wait for emergency evacuation in the morning. I quickly consulted my textbook, *Atlas of Surgical Operations.*

I gave the woman a spinal anesthetic. We proceeded with the incision and soon had a healthy, crying baby. So far so good, but when the placenta came free, blood welled up from her abdomen like an incoming tide. There were no specific bleeders to tie off; the blood just came from everywhere. Things looked bleak. I have never felt so apprehensive in my life, and I was sure we would lose her.

We each got a large, hot, moist towel and pressed down hard. We must have kept the pressure up for 20 of the longest minutes I have ever known before we eased off and gradually removed the towels. Miraculously, the bleeding had stopped and we were able to sew up the incision without incident.

It occurred to me later that I ought to have tied off her tubes to prevent such an event in the future, but as far as I know she did not become pregnant again.

Break between surgeries at Tofino Hospital. I am on the right, and Dr. Arthur Moody is standing between two Aussie nurses. The three of them worked at the hospital for a while in the late 1960s.

Pacific Rim Park

Shortly after eight o'clock one stormy night (why is it that bad things always seem to happen on stormy nights?), I was called to see a woman who had just arrived by boat from the Native community of Ahousat. She was about 50 and had been vomiting copious amounts of blood. I diagnosed ruptured veins in her esophagus as the cause of the bleeding and started her on an IV (her hemoglobin had dropped to a third of the normal level). For many technical reasons it was impossible to have a blood bank in Tofino, and the weather precluded our flying her out to be transfused, which was the only treatment that stood a chance to save her life. What could I do?

I had been in Tofino about four years by this time and had given prenatal care to over 200 Native women. As part of this care, everyone had blood drawn to ascertain their blood group. Without exception, all tested O positive. This suggested to me that there was a strong genetic influence at work. Ordinarily the universal donor is O negative, but in this case I felt that O positive would be safe. I proceeded to the beer parlour at the Maquinna Hotel, where I explained the situation. Three young Native men were more than willing to come back to the hospital with me, and each donated a pint of blood, which we immediately started transfusing into our patient. A nurse was stationed by the bedside, alert for any negative reaction to the transfusion. Fresh blood is better than stored blood for its ability to stop bleeding, and this soon came to pass. All the pints were successfully transfused without incident.

The next morning we were able to send out her blood sample by plane to the Red Cross, which immediately grouped her, cross-matched four pints and flew them back. When we attempted to give her those, she had a reaction to three out of the four. Someone had surely been watching over our shoulders the night before!

The day of my twice-weekly visit to Ucluelet started in its usual way. I stopped at the only gas station in the area, which was run by Ed and Stella Knight. They were busy gardeners, and there weren't many cars, so you had to pump your own gas and write down on a blackboard how much you'd pumped. They kept track of purchases, and when you could connect with them, you paid what was owing.

I continued over the miserable, potholed, washboard road to Ukee. My car was known to everyone, and I was hailed by an elderly Italian gentleman named Fritz Bonnetti. He told me that he had an old dog whose hind legs wouldn't work; they dragged behind him. Fritz couldn't bring himself to shoot his dog and asked if I would give the dog an injection to put him out of his misery.

I had never done such a thing before but agreed to do it after office hours the next time I visited Ucluelet. I thought about what I would use and decided morphine would do the trick. A good-sized dose of morphine was a quarter of a grain, so I gave him ten times that amount.

The actual procedure was a messy affair. We both had to hold the dog down. A tourniquet does not fit well over a dog's hind leg, but I finally got a vein and gave the lethal injection. Fritz thanked me profusely, and off home I went.

Three days later, on my next visit, I saw Fritz, stopped and asked how the burial had gone. He replied that the dog was not dead. He slept for 24 hours, and when he woke up, his back legs worked just fine.

Subsequent research revealed that dogs have a hugely greater tolerance to morphine than humans. Henceforth I used a combination of muscle relaxant and sodium pentothal, which worked. I think I did this about twice more before realizing that a bullet in the head was a far more humane method.

When it came time for our family dog, Tigger, to depart, he and I went off together into the woods. This is an event that should involve only a man and his dog.

≡≡

Tom Gibson was one of the three men who met me at the airport in June 1954 and suggested that I come to Tofino. I had no idea then what a commanding presence he was in the village. He had only a grade-school education, but I would guess his IQ was north of 140. He and his four sons, Ken, David, Gary and Keith, were Gibson Contracting. About the only thing they didn't do was carpentry. Tom kept the whole show going while holding any sibling rivalry in check.

Tom knew where every pipe in Tofino's primitive water system was located, and he was always right there to repair the numerous leaks. There was no sewer system then, and septic tanks were a constant problem and a constant source of revenue for Gibson Contracting. Tom joked that he was ideally suited for this work as he had severe nasal polyps, which virtually eliminated his sense of smell. Nasal polyps are a miserable condition, and other than surgical removal, which afforded only temporary relief, there was no effective remedy at that time.

Tom was either mayor or on council much of the time I lived in Tofino. He was the most civic-minded of men, a great promoter of Tofino and active in the Tofino Chamber of Commerce. He and his boys got most of the town's work for the very good reason that, being local, they could do it better and cheaper than others. This didn't sit too well with some locals, which seemed to me rather petulant. Tom won 99 percent of the big jobs that were put up for contract, and we were all winners as we got the lowest price.

He was the officially appointed coroner as well, though he always referred to himself as the "coronator," investigating accidental deaths and supplying caskets, large, medium and small.

The only obvious impairment caused by his lack of education was his famous mispronunciations, which were often appropriated by his admirers without any suggestion of disrespect, but rather endearment. I frequently found myself referring to "architexts," the end of the "physical year" (when I was doing my bookkeeping), and, of course, the "coronator."

Tom and Daphne always had a New Year's Eve party that was open to everyone in the area. Half the town usually attended; we all brought booze and some wives brought snacks. It was by far the best and liveliest party of the year. After one such party, someone with an urgent problem banged on the front door at 4 a.m. Tom's house was constructed in such a way that to get from the bedroom to the front door, you had to go through the living room, and Tom "almost couldn't get there for all the 'derbis,'" as he put it. I don't know of any Tofinoite of the era who ever referred to "debris" as such after that.

This gift found itself in the next generation. One of his boys was once describing the care and maintenance of his hot tub, explaining how important it was to maintain the correct balance so as to keep the "micro orgasms" in check.

My closest association with Tom was, of course, in his role as chairman of the Tofino hospital board. As medical superintendent, I attended all the board meetings and can attest to how astutely and fairly he handled complex matters affecting the hospital and its staff.

A few years after I arrived in Tofino, having a good hospital came to benefit him more than he would ever have expected. I had just started the day's office consultations in Ucluelet when I got a call from the hospital. Ruby Bernard, a crackerjack surgical nurse, said, "I think you had better get back here right away. We have just admitted Tom Gibson with acute abdominal pain and he looks really ill." I can't remember, but she may have said that it looked like appendicitis. She was a good diagnostician as well as being a super surgical assistant, so I told her to get the operating room ready, picked up my car at the garage (it was always in the garage on Ucluelet day) and hightailed it back.

Tom was in bed and looked very sick. According to his recounting of events, the abdominal pain had come on suddenly and progressed quickly. Tom was in great pain, and his abdomen was hard as a board from peritonitis. It was obviously a case of a ruptured appendix, so we readied him for surgery immediately. Because he did hard physical labour, he had firm, strong abdominal muscles and also a bit of a pot belly, all of which meant that we would be working at the bottom of a deep hole to get at his appendix. For this reason, with Ruby assisting, I opened the abdomen with a paramedian incision that gave us more room to work. We found pus and a black, gangrenous, burst appendix. We removed the appendix, inserted a large drain to allow pus to escape from the abdomen and sewed up the incision. We had done our job.

When an appendix bursts and the abdomen fills with pus, the normal movement of the bowel, called peristalsis, stops. No fluid given by mouth is absorbed, and no gas or feces are passed rectally, so it is necessary to put a suction tube down into the stomach, supply fluids intravenously and also supply massive doses of antibiotics to combat the infection. In most cases the bowel starts functioning and gas is passed within a couple of days, so each morning I would put a stethoscope on Tom's abdomen, hoping to hear the tinkle of bowel sounds, and would ask, "Have you passed any gas?"

One day came and went, two days, then three and we were all as nervous as hell. This was the Chairman of the Board! The fourth morning I went in and Tom had a big grin on his face. When I asked, "Any gas?" he replied, "No," but he rolled down the sheet and there was the biggest, loveliest stool I had ever seen. Crisis resolved.

When I think back to that day, there is no doubt in my mind that if we had tried to send him out, the delay would have been fatal.

I have described a few events with good outcomes; unfortunately, one must also confront one's failures.

On another of those dark and stormy nights, I was called out of bed to see the wife of a young carpenter. She was the daughter of one of the longstanding Tofino families, and she and her husband were just starting out. They lived in a really small house and I found her lying in bed in obvious discomfort.

She was seven months pregnant and had pain in her lower right quadrant. There were two possibilities: a kidney infection or early appendicitis. A urine sample will usually help distinguish between the two, so I collected a sample, took it up to the hospital and, sure enough, found a good supply of pus cells. This seemed to indicate the problem was a kidney infection. I administered an antibiotic and went home.

I did know, however, that sometimes an acutely inflamed appendix will press against the tube that connects the kidney to the bladder, and this can also produce pus in the urine, so I was not completely surprised when her husband phoned two hours later and asked me to see her again as the pain was much worse. Thank God he did.

When I re-examined the woman, she had what we call rebound tenderness, a classic sign of acute appendicitis. We removed an acutely inflamed appendix and all seemed well. Unfortunately, the trauma caused her to go into labour, and she delivered a baby girl two months before term.

The baby was immediately placed in the incubator, progressed normally and was eventually sent home. The parents soon sensed that something was wrong, however, and took the child to a specialist, who told them the baby was blind. What we did not know at the time was that excess oxygen can cause blindness in premature babies. The incubators in those days were primitive, and the oxygen concentrations were difficult to regulate. We were fortunate that this was our only case.

I have relived that rainy night a million times and wonder what might have happened if I had made the correct diagnosis the first time.

Another incident that has haunted me involved my own family. Lynn was pregnant with our fourth child after having had three healthy boys. The early months of this pregnancy were not going well. She had fatigue, nausea and vomiting and was not sleeping. One afternoon, two drug sales reps visited my office, promoting recent drug discoveries and offering samples. One had a new drug that specifically alleviated the problems of early pregnancy. I brought this new drug home with considerable satisfaction, sure that it would help a lot, and it did. Unfortunately, the name of this drug was thalidomide.

When the baby was due, Lynn went out to Port Alberni, where she stayed with our good friend Dr. Bud Lott and his wife, Pat. Bud called to let me know that we had a baby daughter. That was the good news. The bad news was that her face was badly deformed, and as we later discovered, she was also badly mentally retarded.

It was a trying time for all of us, especially Lynn, who was trying to look after three small boys and a daughter who required special care. My mother, God bless her, offered to look after our daughter, who was subsequently institutionalized and died young. Lynn was the only woman I gave these samples to. The guilt if I had given them to others would have been more than I could bear.

Four

Perils of the Deep

Living on the ocean is a joy that relatively few experience. Lynn and I were lucky to live on waterfront property for most of our time in Tofino. Spending time on or in the water, on the other hand, can be perilous. One of the most dangerous occupations is commercial fishing, and I patched up more than a few fishermen at the hospital. Two good friends went out and never came back.

It's not just fishermen who are at risk. Rogue waves and rip currents await the unwary, and getting to people injured at sea can be an adventure. One call came in around 4 a.m. This was when Shell Oil was drilling offshore from Tofino, and I was told that a workman at the Shell drilling platform had fallen and injured his head. They were afraid to move him because they feared an injury to his neck and possibly his spinal cord.

I made the short drive to the airport and boarded the chopper that serviced the oil rig. We flew for about half an hour and landed uneventfully on the rig. Only then was I told that the patient was not on the oil rig itself but on a tender boat far below. I was lowered over the side by winch on a platform called a Billy Pugh (named for the company that makes it), which consisted of a flat disk with ropes rising from spots around the circumference of the disk and attaching to the central cable that was connected to the winch. You stood on the outside of the platform and grabbed the ropes on either side of you to steady yourself and keep you on the disk. I was scared as hell, but we were safely lowered to the stern of the tender, which was bobbing up and down erratically in ten-foot swells.

I was directed to the patient, who was lying on the floor of the engine room. He had a large laceration on his skull, which had bled profusely, but there was not the faintest evidence of any neck injury. I sensed that a competent first-aid attendant would have known this and was just covering his ass.

We bandaged the laceration and loaded the worker onto a stretcher. Now we had to get all of us up to the deck of the rig.

There was lots of slack in the hoist line, which made it easy to load the stretcher on the Billy Pugh. The rest of us who were going up took our places on the disk and grabbed the ropes. Now came the tricky part. The winch operator had to get the line taut just as the stern was near its high point on the wave. He then had to rev the winch at full speed to lift us free of the stern.

The winch started, we lifted up several feet, and then the winch malfunctioned and stopped. The stern fell away from us, but when the next wave crested it rose again and gave us a whack. We hung on for dear life, wondering what was coming next. Luckily, the winch sprang to life and got us the hell out of there.

I wrote Shell a rather uncomplimentary letter about the incident but never got a reply.

≡≡≼

Lynn and I became acquainted with a helicopter pilot who one day offered to take us for a spin down the coast. We were flying low, just south of Long Beach, when we observed a series of pools on top of rocky cliffs that rose 20 to 30 feet above the ocean. We landed and got out to explore.

When we tasted the water and found it salty, we wondered how this was possible when the ocean was so far below us. It didn't take us long to discover the answer to our question. Suddenly the ocean rose up 30 feet and crashed along the surface where we were standing. We ran pell-mell away from the advancing surf, but it caught up with Lynn and rolled her over the rocks, badly injuring her back. She was able to hang on to an outcrop, so was not dragged into the ocean as the wave receded. Fortunately the chopper was parked on higher ground. We reached it in a hurry and were out of there as quickly as possible.

We did not soon forget our experience with a rogue wave. Every year or two, the newspapers report that an unsuspecting tourist has been swept off the rocks and out to sea.

⇒≈⇐

During my summers at Emma Lake as a child, I became a good swimmer and subsequently was a member of the swimming teams at the University of Alberta and the University of Manitoba. This led to some overconfidence. The ocean is no swimming pool.

One day, Ron McLeod, Gary Gibson and I decided to try surfing. A group of us, including wives and friends, drove down to the south end of Long Beach, in front of the original Wickaninnish Inn. There was a substantial surf, which was breaking close to shore. It turned out I was the only one who made it through the shore break into the rollers. I was able to get up on my board, but I soon lost my balance and also lost my board.

No problem, I thought. All I needed to do was swim to shore. I swam hard for five minutes, but when I looked up I found I was twice as far from shore as when I started. I realized that I was caught in some kind of current and couldn't swim forward. I looked to my right, where the waves were crashing on rocks encrusted with sharp barnacles. Getting out that way was out of the question.

While I was mulling my options, the crowd on shore realized that someone was missing and that it was me. Because of the high surf, they couldn't see me in the water. Tom Gibson, Gary's dad, was the one who had to tell Lynn that I was the missing surfer.

Since I couldn't swim for shore or get past the rocks, my only option was to go to the left and try to get to the big rollers so I could bodysurf in. I started swimming again, and after another five minutes I looked up to find I had gone at least twice as far as I should have gone. I was moving with the current now, instead of against it, and I was able to bodysurf to shore.

I learned later that I had done what you are supposed to do if you get caught in a riptide. I survived by good luck, not panicking, and wearing a wetsuit top.

$$\Longrightarrow\Longleftarrow$$

Several years later, after we had moved away from Tofino, we built a cabin on Shell Beach and kept a 12-foot aluminum boat tethered in front of the cabin to use when we visited. Lynn was leery of venturing out in such a small boat, but one day I persuaded her to come out with me to Whaler Island. This is a small island off Tofino that consists of two rocky outcroppings about 400 feet apart, connected to each other by a gorgeous sand spit. A particularly attractive succulent plant grew there, and I wanted to see if I could transplant some of it to Shell Beach.

We set out with a bucket and a shovel and were soon pulling the boat well up on the sandy spit. I had looked at the tide book before we left, and I thought we were at or near high tide, so I was sure the boat would be high and dry. We left the bucket in the boat and proceeded over a sandy ridge to the far side of the spit, shovel in hand, in search of the plant, which we soon found. I asked Lynn to stay there while I went back to retrieve the bucket.

As I reached the top of the ridge, I could see the boat floating offshore. I ran down the short distance to the beach. The boat was tantalizingly close, lazily drifting. I told myself, "You're a really good swimmer. Dive in and grab the boat." Then a saner voice said, "This is how people die, with the wind and current keeping it just out of reach." This tug-of-war continued for seconds that seemed like hours, but I finally let the boat drift away. Now I had to face the music and tell Lynn of our predicament.

Fortunately it was a hot, sunny day, so we didn't have to worry about keeping warm or sheltered. Instead, we could try to come up with ways of attracting help. We found a 40-gallon oil drum and a big stick to beat on it, as well as a large orange tarp that we could wave. Fishing boats went by in the adjacent channel, but none saw our flag or heard our drum. A plane went by and waggled its wings, and we thought the pilot would alert the coast guard, but when dusk came it dawned on us that we would be spending the night on the island.

Lynn smoked at that time and had a lighter with which we started a driftwood fire. We had not brought any food with us but noticed large numbers of mussels clinging tenaciously to the rocks. We knocked several off the rocks with our shovel and roasted them over the fire on the shovel blade. The heat caused the mussels to open up, and we were able to get at the meat, along with several grains of sand. It was not the most satisfying meal we ever had, but it was one of the most appreciated, and the driftwood fire kept at least one side of us warm that night.

The next day began with a dense fog. We were without water, but there was a heavy dew on the sea grass, which I was able to squeeze off between my fingers into a plastic cup we had found. I presented this cup full of muddy water to Lynn, who took one look at it and declined. We set off on a search for water, and on one of the rocky humps found a little pond, about a foot square, brimming with mosquito larvae. At least it was fresh water.

About noon, the fog began to lift. It was low tide, so there was a big expanse of sand dune, and I wrote MAYDAY in 30-foot letters with a sharp stick. A low-flying float plane saw our message and was able to land and retrieve us. We never did go back to get the succulent, and I took a lot of ribbing for not knowing when it was high tide.

Five

Tofino Life

In Tofino, as in other small towns, every resident's character, warts and all, was known to everyone else. Your financial condition or marital status was known by the whole town, literally within minutes. All telephone calls went through a local operator, who had the ability to listen in—not exactly a secure line. To prove that point, my crab-fishing friend Bill White would purposely concoct a lurid, far-fetched tale, which he transmitted by phone in order to reap the satisfaction of hearing it repeated around town as gospel a few hours later. The upshot of this is that characters whose often-hilarious exploits remain unknown in cities are exposed for all to enjoy in small towns.

There was no shortage of characters or incidents in Tofino, which was the year-round home of many fishermen. At the time, they were mostly operating day boats, leaving port early in the morning and returning late at night. A number of extraordinarily successful fishermen had earned the respect of their peers and were known as highliners.

One such fisherman was a good-looking, prematurely grey-haired bachelor, Jimmy Gorgeson, often referred to as the Old Grey Fox. All spring, summer and fall, Jimmy fished hard and usually made a bundle.

During the winter he would rent a room at the Maquinna Hotel and play just as hard. The proximity of the beer parlour proved irresistible, and he spent much time enjoying the camaraderie of local drinkers. It was widely believed among the locals that the annual budget for the Maquinna Hotel was not finalized until it was determined how good a fishing season Jimmy had had.

The Maquinna was the first hotel and liquor outlet in Tofino. It was built and owned by two men, Frank Bull and Dennis Singleton. Dennis ran the hotel and Frank ran the school bus. Neither had much of a sense of humour, and Frank, in fact, had a volatile temper. For a time they had no competition. Then some locals banded together and built a branch of the Canadian Legion, which was licensed for members. Dennis did not view this development kindly, and a certain amount of bad blood arose between the two establishments.

To gain a leg up on the competition, Dennis bought a myna bird for the Maquinna Pub. It had a limited but colourful vocabulary. It seems this presented a challenge to Jimmy, who, having countless hours at his disposal and limitless patience, proceeded over the winter to teach the bird to say "Go to the Legion."

It is an understatement to say that Dennis was not amused by this feat, and the bird soon found itself in new surroundings.

＝＝

The winters in Tofino, while lovely and mild, with no snow to shovel, had the downside of many, many, grey, rainy days, which severely limited outside activities. My father had been a curler in Prince Albert, and I had enjoyed watching him, especially during bonspiels. I thought what a boon it would be to have a curling rink in Tofino to brighten up those winter nights. There were two large airplane hangars left over from World War II, one of which was large enough to accommodate a rink. It was ideally situated midway between Tofino and Ucluelet.

I started talking it up among friends and patients and soon had a core of enthusiastic volunteers. We held some informal organizational meetings and formed the Long Beach Curling Club, a non-profit association, and began to sell memberships. George Gudbranson and Harry Taylor from Ucluelet and Neil Botting of Tofino were active in the association, which was lucky because we had a multitude of hurdles to overcome.

First, we couldn't begin to cool the whole hangar down, so we designed a plastic enclosure within the hanger to contain the cold air.

Curling was popular on the prairies, and there was a three-year waiting time to get curling stones from Scotland. Enter Dad in Edmonton. He did some extensive sleuthing and found a three-rink project that didn't go ahead, and we were able to obtain the rocks ordered for it.

Next we had to physically construct the refrigeration equipment and distribution along three sheets of curling ice. Without the skills of George Gudbranson, an excellent mechanic who donated countless hours of his time, this project would never have come to fruition. But come it did, with membership almost evenly split between Tofino and Ucluelet.

Curling is a game that inspires intense competition, but when the game is over, that rivalry is immediately forgotten, to be replaced, over a few beers, with warm feelings of camaraderie and good will. I mention this because, without our intending it, establishing the curling club went a long way to heal the bitterness that existed after the two towns' long fight over the location of the hospital. It drew residents of Tofino and Ucluelet together in a way we had never expected.

However, just because we got it started didn't mean we were out of the woods. The cost of the electricity needed to produce and maintain ice in such a mild climate was inordinate, and we needed to find some way to supplement annual dues. For a number of years the

Vancouver Flying Club organized a fly-in to the Tofino airport on the July 1 long weekend. Flying clubs from all over British Columbia and the United States participated. A highlight of this event was the crab feed. Tofino was known far and wide for its delectable Dungeness crabs, so the curling club undertook to provide (for a price) a meal of cooked crab and barbecued salmon for the aviators. We also sponsored a hangar dance, for which we hired a good outside band. The dance featured the longest bar in Canada, stretching the whole length of the hangar. It was staffed by ten bartenders, all volunteer curlers. This was our big money-maker for the year, and it allowed the club to stay in business.

Part of the deal for the band was that we would put them up for the night after they had finished playing. On one occasion it fell to Lynn and me to put them up. After the dance, a group of curlers came back to our house along with the band. We were all pretty pumped up over the success of the evening and wanted to continue to party and dance. The bandleader allowed as how they would be only too happy to play for us, but they couldn't because they lacked a piano. What he was really thinking was "We want to get to bed, but this is a dandy excuse because where in hell are they going to get a piano at two o'clock in the morning?" He hadn't taken into account the ingenuity and resolve of West Coasters.

My good friend Gary Gibson (one of Tom's boys) happened to have brought his pickup truck. We all put our heads together and agreed that Chris (Green) Douglass had a piano. At one time Chris had been my secretary, but then she studied radiography and became the x-ray technician at the hospital. We shared the curse of being on call 24 hours a day, and chances were that if I were called out, about half the time I would have to phone her to come in and do an x-ray. Although this was an onerous intrusion, she always came in with a smile and uncomplaining attitude. She was a joy to work with and I considered her a great friend.

Left to right: Ruth White, Gail Miles and Chris (Green) Douglass.

Anyway, on the night of the hangar dance, seven or eight of us exploded out of my house and knocked on Chris's door. We explained to the young surprised babysitter who opened it that Chris wouldn't mind if we borrowed her piano, which we proceeded to do. It was light as a feather. We arrived back at our house and triumphantly rolled in the piano. The look of unhappiness on the faces of the band members was unmistakable, but they did play for about half an hour. The party soon ran out of steam and everybody went to bed.

The next morning brought a sombre reality. It was apparent that Chris, tolerant as she was, was not one bit amused. The group of piano movers from the night before was reassembled, hungover and contrite, and proceeded to lift the heaviest piano on earth onto Gary's truck. Chris opened the door, no smile, body language that spelled anger, and we deposited the piano and fled.

Repairs were needed, as well as retuning, which we gladly paid for. If anything falls under the heading of "It Seemed Like a Good Idea at the Time," this was it.

Chris gradually forgave us, but it was at least ten years before we could both laugh about it.

＝＝＝

George Pownall was a delightful man who occupied a nondescript house called Wits End. The land it sat on was far from nondescript, as it included hundreds of feet of waterfront on Chesterman Beach and Shell Beach, as well as extensive frontage on Tofino Inlet.

Just after I arrived in Tofino in 1954, Chesterman Beach, about three miles south of Tofino, caught my eye. You arrived on the beach via a trail through rainforest that opened onto Chesterman's southern end. Once on the beach walking north, you passed a sandy spit stretching out to Frank Islands and continued north to a rocky headland about 30 feet above the sand. When I stood there for the first time, the words "one day" echoed in my mind. When I had worked at the Banff Springs Hotel in the summers during medical school, I had inadvertently been bitten by the hotel bug. In all my dreams I could not imagine a more spectacular site for a resort hotel, and I came to covet this property with a passion.

When I got to know George, I would approach him about buying his Chesterman Beach land. He knew I didn't have the money and was not a serious prospect, but he would always name a price. I think he started out asking $60,000, which was way out of my league, and each year, like clockwork, the asking price would escalate by $10,000. One year the market dived, and I was sure the price would go down from the previous year's $90,000, maybe to $80,000, but when I asked, the price had gone up by its usual $10,000 to $100,000. I expressed my surprise, and George replied, "I might as well not sell it at $100,000 as not sell it for $80,000."

I took this picture of Chesterman Beach in the 1960s. I was lying on the floor of the baggage compartment of a small plane and shooting the picture through the open baggage compartment door. Shell Beach and the future sites of the new Wickaninnish Inn and my family's cabin are just off the left edge of the photo. There are now over 100 homes on or adjacent to Chesterman Beach..

I first got to know George because his wife was dying of breast cancer and needed shots to be administered by the local doctor. When she died, George found a number of local ladies who enjoyed pouring him a morning cup of coffee—this was referred to as "George's rounds." He was good company, and I believe he supported himself with a small pension. He also hired people to pick ferns and salal, which he packaged and sold to florists. He lived modestly and didn't require a large income.

One evening we were all gathered for a party at Chris Douglass's. She was someone who could ordinarily keep a secret, but this night she announced that she knew something we all didn't know and that it would shock the hell out of us. No amount of entreaty would make her divulge anything until I asked if it involved vital statistics. Thinking the question innocuous, she said yes. No one could predict death, and I knew who was pregnant, which left only marriages. We soon ascertained that George Pownall had recently bought a new pair of shoes and, further, he was missing. No one knew where he had gone or when he would be back. It all clicked. Pownall had run away to get married. We had no inkling who the bride might be. Notwithstanding this, we felt she was entitled to a "Welcome to Tofino" event.

The local troublemakers soon arrived at George's house in a truck, opened the front door and proceeded to remove *all* the furniture save two chairs. We took the truck and furniture and parked it in an unused hangar at the airport. We also discovered that the local RCMP constable was meeting the bride and groom at the airport and transporting them home.

Shortly after their return, Jack Walter and I dropped by to pay our respects. The bride, Terry, was seated serenely in her chair, looking not the least bit discomfited, as though this was the most normal reception in the world. Talk about aplomb.

When our wives heard the news, they were outraged at our treatment of the bride and booked the bridal suite at the Maquinna Hotel for George and Terry. The rooms and meals were on us for the next three days, as rain kept us from retrieving the furniture.

George later sold his property to a group of Americans for $133,000, bought a sporty red convertible and retired to Victoria.

Six

Politics or It's a Good Thing We Don't Get All the Government We Pay For

My interest in politics began when I was a teenager in the early 1940s. As I mentioned earlier, we lived in Prince Albert, Saskatchewan, and our next-door neighbours were the Harradences, Herb, Celia and their two sons, Milt and Clyne. Herb was a good friend of John Diefenbaker, the local member of Parliament and later prime minister of Canada, who would regale us all with tales from Ottawa, the first taste of trouble to come. My father was a banker, and I think his occupation had something to do with my conservative politics. One thing it did do was reduce my fear of bankers.

In Tofino there were two political bodies, an active Chamber of Commerce and the town council. I became a member of the Chamber soon after I arrived on the coast, and a few years later I was elected one of the seven town councillors.

Tofino was in the federal Comox-Alberni riding and the provincial Alberni constituency. Both were held by the NDP and were generally reckoned to be unassailable. Control of the legislature in

Victoria, however, rested with the Social Credit Party (Socreds) under the firm hand of W.A.C. Bennett. During at least two elections, the Socred candidate had made sporadic, aimless appearances in Tofino, looking like a lost dog. No one rented a hall or organized a meeting for him, and he inevitably lost.

In early 1966, with another election in the wind, I called on Paul Kimola, a local entrepreneur who ran the sawmill he had built himself. I knew he was a card-carrying Socred. Together we formed a local branch of the party and sold at least 30 memberships. Whoever the candidate, he was going to get a lot more support than in the past. We asked the party brass in Victoria to send us a speaker to kick-start things, and Herb Bruch, the MLA from Esquimalt, came out and gave a rousing stump speech.

Campaigning in Opitsat, 1966. I am standing between Harry Masso and his granddaughter Barbara (Babs). Harry was a delightful old gentleman, a long-time patient and resident of Opitsat. Babs was always a bright spark.

Campaigning in Port Alberni with my three sons, Bruce, Charles and Jim. JIM RYAN PHOTO

Most of us met afterward at the Maquinna Hotel for a B.S. session, and Herb said to me, "Why don't you consider running?"

I was completely taken aback and told him how wildly unlikely it was that someone from Tofino, population 500, could get the nomination, let alone win the seat, when there were 30,000 people residing in the Albernis (Alberni and Port Alberni), which was an NDP stronghold.

Herb calmly replied, "A strong candidate can win anywhere."

When I got home and recounted this episode to Lynn, she gave me a steely look and said, "I married you for better or for worse, but not for politics."

My latent love for politics bloomed irresistibly, however, and after consulting with two good friends—Ron Burley, a realtor from Ucluelet, and Jack Walter, a grocery store owner from Tofino—I decided to go for the nomination. We visited everyone who had a Socred card and promised to put on a crackerjack campaign if I were the candidate. Enthusiasm was high, and somehow we won the nomination over five other hopefuls on the first ballot. The nomination meeting was the first time I met Dan Campbell, minister of Municipal Affairs, who represented the adjacent constituency in the Comox Valley. He would remain a lifelong friend.

The most prominent plank in our election campaign was the establishment of a national park centred on Long Beach, an idea that had been kicking around for a few years. Back in 1963, Arthur Laing, the federal member for Vancouver South and minister responsible for parks, had floated a trial balloon that suggested spending $10 million on a national park around Mount Garibaldi, north of Vancouver. The Tofino Chamber of Commerce immediately denounced the idea, pointing out that Canada already had enough mountain parks, including Mount Revelstoke, Kootenay, Glacier and Yoho in British Columbia. The provincial Recreation minister at that time, Earle Westwood, agreed with the Tofino Chamber's position that a seaside park should be established instead.

Tom Gibson was the driving force in the Tofino Chamber, and he told the members that it didn't really matter what resolutions Tofino passed; they needed to be adopted as a top or second priority by the Vancouver Island Chamber of Commerce before they would gain the attention of government. Through persistent lobbying we convinced the Vancouver Island Chamber to adopt these priorities, and in 1964 both Tom and I attended a Chamber meeting with Ken Kiernan, the new Recreation minister. Kiernan agreed that a coastal park was a good idea and promised to submit it to cabinet. However, in Paul St. Pierre's *Vancouver Sun* column in February 1966, Tom Gibson lamented that there had been no response to this idea for over a year and a half.

There were rumours that the Chamber had been told indirectly that the provincial cabinet did not favour turning the land over to the federal government for development. Art Laing and W.A.C. Bennett had been adversaries in the BC legislature, and there was little love lost between them. Given that W.A.C. had little love for the feds at the best of times, it's safe to say he was not disposed to handing them large swatches of pristine BC coastline, especially if Arthur Laing would be making political hay out of it.

The process of creating a park around Long Beach had obviously become dormant and needed someone with some clout to kick-start it. I saw myself as that person and campaigned relentlessly on this issue when I became the Social Credit candidate in the 1966 provincial election.

The campaign was a barnburner. We didn't expect to win, but we ran to win. Ron Burley raised over $18,000, which was more than any other candidate collected, including Herb Capozzi, who was a successful businessman in the high-profile Vancouver Centre constituency. Jack Walter was my superb campaign manager. We put on free salmon barbecues and greeted workmen at the end of midnight shifts, and no beer parlour was safe from us. We also had a secret weapon, Rudy Boyce and his band, which we hired to travel the whole constituency, from Bowser to Bamfield and Tahsis. No whistle stop was too obscure.

Rudy is a story by himself. In the early spring of 1966, Jack and Sylvia Walter and Lynn and I took a vacation and visited several Caribbean Islands. While in Trinidad, we heard Rudy sing and thought he was spectacular, so much so that Jack became his manager and brought him to Canada. His first gig was at Bob Wright's Oak Bay Marina in Victoria, where he meshed flawlessly with the incumbent band. He filled the place to overflowing for weeks on end. One day we were walking down the street with Rudy after we had spent over $1,000 on his wardrobe. He turned and looked at each of us and said, "You guys are going to have to dress better if you want to hang out with me!"

Rudy and his band would warm up the audience before the boring political speeches. My opponent, John Squire of the NDP, thought we were gaining an unfair political advantage. He became even more incensed when we offered Rudy to sing at the Grade 12 grad dance, where his daughter was one of the students graduating.

Thanks to Rudy and my Long Beach park plank—as well as the salmon barbecues I hosted and my visits to local beer parlours—we were creating a buzz in the constituency, and Bill Budd, W.A.C.'s principal secretary, who was visiting, phoned the campaign headquarters and said, "These guys are just crazy enough to win!" As a result, W.A.C. agreed to come and speak.

We rented the high school auditorium, which was packed, and W.A.C. and I walked arm in arm down the aisle to the podium to the tune of "When the Saints Go Marching In." John Squire's comment was "He may be a lot of things, but he sure as hell is no saint."

We won the election by just over 1,700 votes, unheard of for a Socred in Alberni. Heady stuff for a country doctor!

Campaigning with Rudy Boyce, 1966.

Seven

Election Promises

So now I had been elected. Maybe that was the easy part. I was the MLA but was still running a full-time medical practice in Tofino, connected to the main centre of population by 70 miles of bad road that was only open between 5 p.m. and 8 a.m. except on weekends, when it was open 24 hours a day.

This road was the subject of one of the three main election promises I had to fulfill.

The easiest to achieve was my promise of better access from Alberni to the east coast of the Island. In 1966, the road from Qualicum Beach on the east coast to Alberni on the west was heavily travelled by logging trucks and the usual kinds of traffic from a large industrial city. The road traversed a low mountain pass, containing severe up-slopes and down-slopes, with numerous tight curves. Traffic often moved at a snail's pace, and it was almost impossible to pass. The solution was relatively simple: construct numerous passing lanes. The district highways manager, Jock McGregor, agreed to make this his priority, and I worked my end through the Highways minister, Phil Gaglardi. We soon had some action.

My second promise, improving Highway 4 from Tofino/Ucluelet to Alberni, proved more difficult. First some history. The Tofino Chamber of Commerce had for years agitated for a road out to Alberni. In the mid- to late 1950s, the provincial government began awarding tree farm licences in the area to logging companies. One licence in Clayoquot Sound was awarded to BC Forest Products (BCFP) on the condition that BCFP build a road around Kennedy Lake. Much of this involved drilling and blasting a steep, sheer rock face to create a barely passable road. When this road was finished, it connected at its northwest end to a logging road owned by the Kennedy Lake Logging Division of MacMillan Bloedel (MacBlo), which in turn connected to the Tofino–Ucluelet Highway.

At the east end of the BCFP section, the province built about 12 miles of gravel road to connect with logging roads owned by MacBlo's Sproat Lake Division. The roads of the Sproat Lake Division contained notorious sets of switchbacks at either end of a high, narrow road that was about ten miles long. If you happened to look out the car window while travelling those ten miles, you saw what looked like an unimpeded thousand-foot plunge into the lake.

All these sections of road were finally cobbled together and opened in 1959. I was in England studying surgery at the time and missed the grand opening caravan. Many of the people who had come to Tofino by road refused to return over it, opting either to fly out or go by boat.

When I returned to the coast, I had more than a few requests for tranquilizers from people who were heading out on the road. Besides the switchback sections and the sheer drop, there were potholes as big as washtubs, and protruding rocks lying in wait to puncture an oil pan. Most locals who had to use the road carried two spare tires, extra oil, food and, in winter, sleeping bags.

Everyone had their favourite horror story of travelling over the Tofino–Alberni road. Mine involved a night during the winter when it was snowing heavily. We had chains, so we made it up the west end of the switchbacks fairly easily, but going downhill on the east end, even with chains, was like going down a ski jump with curves. We were all shaken when we got to Port Alberni, and I phoned Ross Ellis, the district highways manager, to tell him how dangerous it was. He agreed to send out a truck and sand the section, but it was so slippery the truck flipped over. They closed the road. When it snowed heavily, the road was often closed.

Another time, Lynn and I sneaked out to have dinner in Port Alberni. Returning late at night, we got a flat. No problem, except the spare (repaired just that morning) was also flat. We were afraid that if we fell asleep, no passing car would stop, so we collected some small tree limbs and small logs and spread them in a line across the road. About two hours later, two fishermen in a pickup truck stopped, although they were apprehensive that we might be robbers. Four of us jammed into the front seat and we made it home just in time for work.

Others vividly recall their experiences with the switchbacks. In August 2008, Les Leyne, the political columnist for the *Victoria Times Colonist*, wrote: "I love the change from the tame east coast of the island to the wild west coast. It's only a few hours but it's a completely different world. The trip over is nice but it was better when it was a rough logging road and your mom is piloting a Beetle past cliffs so close to the edge that she has to pull over every so often and have a cry. Now that's adventure." That's more like it.

Soon after I was elected, I agreed to speak at a luncheon of the board of trade in Port Alberni. I had recently bought a Land Rover to cope with the road. It had been raining for several days, and Kennedy Lake had risen. There was one notorious low spot on the way around the lake, and water had completely covered the road. Even though the Rover was pretty high off the ground, I wasn't sure I could make it through. There was only one thing to do: I stripped down to my underwear and waded in. It didn't seem *too* deep, so I went back to the Rover and drove on through. It made a good story, and the board of trade members appreciated the lengths I had gone to in order to attend the meeting.

The obvious solution to the problem was to relocate the switch-back section around Sproat Lake, but that was no easy task. There was no existing road allowance, so I was directed to Norm Zapf, who was in charge of locations for the Ministry of Highways. He agreed to allocate a corner of his budget to see if it was physically possible to relocate the road. This took a year. I then went to talk to people in charge of rights of way so they could check out ownership along the proposed route and ascertain if the government could obtain land for the road and under what cost or condition. This took another year. Then the ministry had to estimate the total cost, including obtaining the rights of way and constructing this section of Highway 4. This took one more year, but at the end of the day I had a number, which proved to be very important for a meeting with W.A.C.

My third promise was probably the most difficult one and involved the creation of a national park centred on Long Beach. In early September 1966, in the midst of the election campaign, Ken Kiernan, the incumbent provincial minister of recreation, offered Art Laing, the federal minister responsible for parks, all British Columbia's holdings in the Long Beach area to form the nucleus of a national park. This offer came out of the blue. As I mentioned earlier, there had been nothing said about the park for a year and a half. Laing responded to this by saying he would act with the speed of light on the offer, but in the next breath he said, "I only wish Mr. Kiernan would carry this attitude through to Garibaldi." Kiernan made it clear that Long Beach was a counter-offer to Garibaldi, and things stalled again.

Getting the park ultimately took even longer than moving Highway 4. In the meantime, I took my seat in the BC legislature.

Eight

The Drinking Man's Friend

After the election, the first sitting of the House, the BC legislature, occurred in January 1967. I received a call beforehand, telling me that I would have the honour of seconding the speech from the throne, which opened the session. Herb Capozzi, the MLA for Vancouver Centre, was called upon to move the speech from the throne. We were chosen because of our unexpected wins in what were previously strong NDP constituencies.

This may seem pretty esoteric to the average reader, but it was of considerable help to me because we were the first and only two members to speak that day, which meant we would get good press coverage. All the papers reported on my call for a West Coast marine park, which I proposed be named after Captain James Cook. I used any opportunity to get support from my fellow Socreds. Ray Perrault, the Liberal leader, and his successor, Pat McGeer, were very much for it because it involved the federal Liberals. Bob Strachan, leader of the NDP, represented an Island constituency, so he came on board. After all, being against parks was like being against motherhood. Only Bob Williams of the NDP had complaints.

I had always wanted to fly and first owned a Cessna 140, a wheels-only aircraft. Because there were more neat places to visit on the west coast that were only accessible by sea, I bought a small amphibious flying boat called a Seabee. After I became an MLA, the plane gave me access to parts of the constituency not accessible by road. Because I used it as a political tool, I called it the Socred II *and painted the name on the hull. "Flying Phil" Gaglardi, the minister of Highways, had a Lear jet, so in brackets below* Socred II *I put "This is not a Lear jet."*

The Socred MLAs elected for the first time in 1966 were an intelligent and talented group who had left thriving businesses to contribute. They were not easily intimidated, except, of course, by the "old man," W.A.C. Bennett, who intimidated everyone without even trying.

All MLAs were assigned seats on the various parliamentary committees. Mine was Municipal Affairs, whose chairman was Waldo Skillings, W.A.C.'s long-time bridge partner and confidant. Waldo was also the party whip, which meant he was responsible for knowing where all his members were and ensuring they could be rounded up and brought into the House to defeat a snap motion from the opposition that could bring the government down.

In February 1967, the Municipal Affairs committee was voting on a series of amendments to the Vancouver Charter that had been submitted by the minister, Dan Campbell. The anomaly in this particular committee was that the chairman (Waldo) could cast a tying vote and then vote again to break the tie. The Socreds had a one-vote margin over the opposition, so it appeared there would be no problem passing Dan's amendments. However, when Waldo called the vote, he voted with the opposition to tie the vote and then proceeded to vote again to defeat the motion.

This embarrassed the minister and made us on the government side look foolish, but Waldo exulted in his power and his ability to show these rookies a thing or two.

The afternoon session was to be followed by an evening session, so a number of us backbenchers went for dinner across the street at the Empress Hotel. Our colleagues who weren't on that particular committee were as incensed as we were by Waldo's action and decided to do something about it.

The evening session started at seven, and Waldo noticed almost no backbenchers were present. Thirty minutes later, W.A.C. asked him where all the backbenchers were. Waldo didn't know, and he was getting more panicky by the minute. Finally, three-quarters of an hour late, we showed up, whereupon Waldo, white as a sheet, started to lecture us on how the government could have fallen, etc., etc.

Instead of being contrite, we proceeded to tell him that we knew full well the risks, but if he ever pulled a stunt like that on a minister again, we would stay out until the government did fall. He was well and truly chastened.

≥≤

As the rookie MLA representing Alberni, I had a fine line to walk. Many people saw the Socreds as right-of-centre pragmatists, but others, especially union executives, believed they were anti-union, right-wing zealots. I tried to position myself as somewhere in the middle and something of a maverick. I personally was never anti-union and during the election campaign in 1966 had decried the union-busting tactics of Noranda Mines at their Brynnor Mine near Ucluelet.

I couldn't always straddle the middle ground, though, and in early 1968 I was tested when severe labour unrest in the forest industry gradually escalated into the threat of a strike by the International Woodworkers of America (IWA). This would have shut down the industry throughout the province, with devastating economic impact on communities and the provincial treasury.

The cabinet felt it had to act and introduced Bill 3, which called for compulsory arbitration. Of course this was anathema to the union and produced a vitriolic response from the NDP in the legislature.

It wasn't long before the Port Alberni IWA local summoned me to appear before the union membership at the union hall and explain my support for such offensive legislation. I knew that my political future depended on how I handled this situation.

I consulted with my Socred constituency executives, and one thing became clear: if I consented to the union's demand that I appear before a completely hostile audience, I would be skinned alive. However, I couldn't duck the issue by simply hunkering down in Victoria.

The solution we came up with was to state that Bill 3 recognized the public at large had an interest bigger than that of the union and the employers. This being the case, the public should be invited to participate in the discussion. My constituency association rented an auditorium in Alberni for a meeting open to all.

I knew this was make or break and was nervous as hell. Before the meeting started, I was backstage at the auditorium when someone told me the IWA local's president wanted to be able to address the crowd. My first reaction was "I hired the hall; go and hire a hall and have your own meeting." Fortunately, one of my long-time supporters,

Dave Russell, was present. He drew me aside and imparted the best political advice I ever got: "Be magnanimous and give him 15 minutes at the start of the meeting. It's important for them to have their say, and they can't complain later of having been shut out."

The IWA agreed to pay half the hall rental, the president had his say for 15 minutes, I outlined my and the government's position, and then I threw the meeting open to questions, which I answered to the best of my ability. The whole thing lasted for a couple of hours. There were no winners, but everyone who wanted to give their opinion was able to participate, and I was given full marks for guts and not ducking.

=≡=

I may have built up some goodwill with the woodworkers with a speech I gave in the House in February 1968, though that same speech upset a few of my colleagues.

It was well known that Premier W.A.C. Bennett and Phil Gaglardi were teetotallers, as were several lesser-known cabinet ministers. Backbenchers soon learned that talking about liquor in a favourable light was a risky proposition, one that could severely mar your chances for political advancement.

However, when the cities of Alberni and Port Alberni amalgamated in October 1967, the BC liquor board shut down both of the new city's liquor stores and opened a lone outlet in a shopping mall, greatly reducing convenience and accessibility. There had been two substantial hikes in the price of liquor in recent years, and the government had just announced an imminent increase in the cost of beer.

I represented a constituency of loggers, miners and fishermen who were often away from home in camps or on boats for long periods of time. When they returned home, they enjoyed the social atmosphere and camaraderie of the beer parlour, which was, in effect, the working man's club. There were a lot more people in my constituency who drank than who didn't drink, and I thought it high time someone said so.

On February 13, 1968, I stood up in the House to speak on behalf of the drinking man. My message was "Enough is enough," and I ended my discussion of drinking with a poem:

> *Here's to the four pillars of virtue,*
> *lying, swearing, stealing and drinking.*
> *When you lie, lie for a pretty girl.*
> *When you steal, steal away from bad company.*
> *When you swear, swear by your country.*
> *And when you drink, drink with me.*

All this seems pretty innocent now, but not then. The press were all agog and I inherited the sobriquet "the drinking man's friend."

In the same speech I indirectly brought up, once again, the need to have Long Beach proclaimed a national park. The context was the Long Beach fly-in, which occurred over the July 1 long weekend each year (this was the event for which the Long Beach Curling Club had organized fundraising crab feeds and hangar dances). The fly-in quickly grew to massive proportions, though most of the participants were now campers arriving by car rather than by plane.

The event had become a zoo and a dangerous one. There was no regulation precluding camping on the beach, driving on the beach, or landing aircraft on the beach. The result was that there had been fatalities involving pedestrians and motor vehicles. There are no centre lines on beaches.

As well, the small provincial campsite at Green Point had only two toilets, which meant long lineups. Many campers gave up on the lineups and went behind the nearest rock or tree.

If the area had been a national park under federal government control, there would have been safety regulations in place and enforced, but the beach was still owned and nominally controlled by the provincial government. My job was to articulate this state of affairs in a way that would not be forgotten. The problem was that the state of affairs involved activities that were commonly described using terms that would be instantly gavelled down by the Speaker of the House. Luckily, I knew the medical terminology.

"Are you aware, Mr. Speaker, that on July 1 of last year there were 7,000 campers tenting on Long Beach provincial park, crammed in cheek by jowl, defecating, micturating and copulating—not separated by so much as a blade of grass, Mr. Speaker? In fact, barely a grain of sand. Motorcycles racing up and down the beach, airplanes landing and taking off, no water and two toilets for 7,000 people."

It had its desired effect. Ian Hunter, writing the next day in the *Vancouver Sun*, said, "The doctor from Alberni riding not only dared to mention booze while his fellow Socreds goggled, but he mentioned defecation, micturition and copulation—terms with which it was evident few of his fellow MLAs and cabinet ministers were familiar. Bennett managed to smile once or twice and even winked to rally his stunned cabinet ministers about him. Even Opposition leader Robert Strachan looked apprehensively a couple of times toward the Speaker's chair while Dr. McDiarmid spoke. But Speaker William Murray—who has cracked down on members for using unparliamentary language repeatedly this session—remained calm, if stern. It was almost as if the clinical sound of some of Dr. McDiarmid's terms made them respectable."

I learned later from my good friend Dan Campbell, who sat immediately behind W.A.C. and Ray Williston, that W.A.C. had leaned over to Williston and asked, "What does copulation mean?"

Williston replied, "I think it's a medical term, sir."

The following year, camping and cars were banned, but the whole episode only increased my feeling that this wonderful beach had to be preserved in its pristine state. I would need to work harder to get national park status.

Nine

First Steps to Pacific Rim Park

During the summer of 1967, staff from the federal parks branch arrived in Tofino to conduct a survey of the proposed park. They tried to remain incognito while they were in the area, not wanting to tarnish their reputation by being seen with a politician. However, in such a small town their cover was soon blown, and the Chamber of Commerce and I offered all the help we could, including introducing them to people who knew the history of the area and providing any transportation they required.

They returned to Ottawa and took some time to prepare a report, which was undoubtedly favourable. I got an inkling from them that the Chamber's vision of the park was too small and that it would evolve to encompass a much larger area.

On the political level, things were not going smoothly. Laing continued to cling to Garibaldi, and I suspect that when Kiernan learned of the proposed boundary expansion, he feared costs would escalate enormously, making it much more difficult to get cabinet approval. At that time, federal policy required the provinces to shoulder the cost of any land acquisition and simply transfer title to the federal government, free and clear. However, British Columbia had no legislative provision for the province to pay for land acquired to become a national park. So we had two powerful elements promoting massive inaction: jockeying politicians and money.

The breakthrough came on July 6, 1968, when Jean Chrétien replaced Art Laing as minister of Indian Affairs and Northern Development with responsibility for Parks Canada. In October, Kiernan wrote to Chrétien and asked if, in his new role, he planned to resume negotiations on the Long Beach proposal. Kiernan went on to say the park would be smaller than originally conceived because British Columbia did not agree with Ottawa's position that the province share in the cost of acquiring land not already held by BC and Canada.

In his response, Chrétien confirmed an earlier Ottawa proposal that the feds would participate in the acquisition of land at Long Beach.

We wanted Chrétien to visit Long Beach so he could experience its remarkable beauty firsthand. It so happened that a Liberal, Richard Durante, represented Alberni federally at that time, and he arranged for Chrétien to visit on November 25, 1968. The Tofino and Ucluelet Chambers of Commerce organized a luncheon at the spectacular Wickaninnish Inn, owned and managed by Robin Fells. The whole length of Long Beach was visible from the hotel lounge, and it was clear that Chrétien was impressed. I acted as MC for the proceedings, welcoming the Quebec MP and minister to the West Coast. We even placed a bet on the upcoming Grey Cup. If the western team won, Chrétien would send me lobster from Nova Scotia, while if the east won, I'd send him Tofino Dungeness crabs. (I lost the bet when Calgary lost a heartbreaker to the Ottawa Rough Riders, 24–21.)

The following day, Chrétien met with Kiernan. Both men were optimistic at the end of their meeting. I heard this with great relief. The park was finally on its way, and both federal and provincial parks staff worked feverishly over the next few months.

In the speech from the throne at the beginning of the 1969 legislative session, the House was asked to "consider legislation to facilitate the development of a National Park on the west coast of Vancouver Island," and on March 20, Kiernan introduced An Act to Authorize the Establishment of a National Park on Vancouver Island. The act received royal assent on April 2 and revealed that several things were falling into place.

1. The act referred to park lands in the Renfrew, Barclay and Clayoquot land districts. We deduced from this that the park would encompass not just Long Beach, but likely the West Coast life-saving trail between Bamfield and Port Renfrew as well. The lands in Barclay district turned out to be the Effingham Islands at the mouth of Barkley Sound, which were largely uninhabited Crown lands belonging to the province.
2. The act also allowed the province to enter into an agreement with the Government of Canada to establish a national park.
3. The act provided for the province to contribute to the cost of the park. It specified that British Columbia would pay half the cost of lands to be acquired. This was a significant compromise for both governments, which up to that point had wanted the other to pay all the costs.
4. The act gave British Columbia power to expropriate lands and to transfer lands acquired by the province to the Government of Canada.
5. Finally, the act froze development within the designated area. This prevented land speculators from coming in and running up the price of land that might be bought or expropriated for the park.

There were three things the act did not do. It did not define the boundaries of the park; it did not create a park, only enabled the province to do so; and it did not set a time frame.

The act did show that British Columbia was serious about establishing this park. I was proud of Ken Kiernan for reacting at light speed once we had the federal minister's interest and support. Now the parks branch could move ahead with the business of assembling the land, defining the boundaries and estimating costs. This last aspect was of considerable concern to me, because if the costs were too high, either party could still withdraw.

During the negotiations over what lands were to be included and how costs would be apportioned, I was invited to a meeting in Ken Kiernan's office attended by both federal and provincial parks people. The Long Beach section of the park was wholly in my constituency, and I was concerned about the owners at the south end of the beach. Their property was unique, and if the government expropriated it, they wouldn't be able to buy a new place that was anything like what they had lost. These holdings made up a small area, and I argued that the owners be given life tenancy. The park would still be there after they died, and at that point their land would become part of the park.

I also wanted the Wickaninnish Inn to be allowed to continue operating. It had a large, loyal clientele in all parts of Canada. The building itself was attractive, and I thought it added to the park rather than detracting from it. After discussion, the feds decided they couldn't abide having private ownership in a national park, so they drew a small circle around the area and excluded it from the park.

At a second meeting some time later, to which I was not invited, this exclusionary zone was erased. The result was that the Wickaninnish Inn was given a limited lease to continue to operate within the park.

During any official discussions about the park, I had to be sure I made no reference to what property should or should not be included in the northern part of the park. This was because in 1962 I had bought property on Chesterman Beach, about three miles north of Radar Hill, a piece of federal Crown land that would surely be included in the park. As long as the government was acquiring private lands, properties north of Radar Hill, including mine, might be deemed appropriate for acquisition. It was a delicate situation and left me vulnerable to political criticism for conflict of interest. Indeed, I was conflicted myself. If my land were taken, it would be at a market price substantially above what I had paid for it. On the other hand, if it were not included, the price would probably rise because there would be less land available for sale, and more people possibly wanting to buy it. From this perspective it was a win-win situation for me, which meant it was a losing situation if someone accused me of conflict of interest. My only hope was that my motive—the desire to create the park—would be seen as overriding personal considerations.

Work on the park was well underway, but the end of the session was in sight, and I was concerned that two of my three promises—the Long Beach park and relocation of Highway 4—were still far from fulfilled.

Ten

One-on-One Meeting with W.A.C.
(My Most Important Meeting as an MLA)

In the late spring of 1969, election fever was in the air. W.A.C. Bennett usually called an election every three years, and the clock was ticking down to the end of the third year.

Bill Budd, the premier's secretary, whom I had first met during the 1966 election campaign, and who was instrumental in having W.A.C. travel to Alberni to speak on my behalf, tapped me on the shoulder. In the course of our conversation, he told me that W.A.C. would be meeting with me over the next few weeks to discuss my re-election prospects and determine what constituency projects were important to me as the MLA. Budd told me that he would wait and arrange the meeting at a propitious time, when the "old man" was in a receptive mood, but that I should make sure I was prepared for it.

This would be the first time I had met W.A.C. one on one except during the election campaign, and I was nervous. Bennett was a powerhouse, a shrewd and fiscally conservative politician who could stretch a dollar a long way. He felt strongly that control of government spending was a priority of his administration. To that end, he was not only the premier, but also the minister of Finance and chairman of the Treasury Board, the body that approved or denied the government's large capital expenditures. He exercised almost complete control of the government through the power of the purse, and I knew that our meeting could make or break the park and my career as an MLA. I wasn't sure how the drinking man's friend would be received.

As promised, a few days later, Bill Budd beckoned me down to the premier's office, ushered me in and left us alone.

I sat down, and W.A.C. said, "Well, what do you need?"

I replied, "Two things."

He said, "What's the first?"

I said, "We need to get the switchback road around Sproat Lake relocated."

He said, "What's it going to cost?"

I was ready for him. The three years of work and research I had put into this problem came to fruition when I told him it would cost $2.3 million.

He immediately picked up the phone and said, "Get me Miard."

Tom Miard was the deputy minister of Highways. When he came on the line, W.A.C. told him I was with the premier in his office, and we needed to know what the relocation around Sproat Lake would cost.

Miard said, "Let me get the file."

When he came back on the line, he said, "Two million four."

W.A.C. said, "It's just had Treasury Board approval" and hung up the phone.

I was elated.

Then he asked me, "What's the second thing?"

I gave a short recitation of how important the park was to me and the constituency and to my getting re-elected.

He looked up at me and said, "*You will get your park*," and the meeting was over.

Many people have attempted to give various individuals, in particular Ken Kiernan and Jean Chrétien, credit for creation of the park, and rightly so, but what they have overlooked is the fact that establishment of Pacific Rim National Park required the expenditure of large amounts of provincial money to acquire private properties. While enabling legislation for the park had been passed, it was by no means certain that it would be funded. With this commitment from the minister of Finance and the chair of Treasury Board, I knew that these expenditures would be approved, which was a giant step forward.

W.A.C. deserves huge credit for this. I believe to this day that if I had not represented a Social Credit constituency, the outcome would have been very different.

When I left the office, I was ecstatic. A short time later, as reality set in, a little internal voice said, "Yes, but we had better win the next election, and I had better win Alberni."

Eleven

Beer on the Beach

A few months later, in the summer of 1969, I was preparing for a camping trip with my family. I had secured the services of a doctor who would come in and take over the practice while I was on holiday. We were leaving first thing in the morning, and my locum had agreed to meet with me at the hospital in the early evening so I could go over problem patients with him. Earlier that day, Nick Seymour, a young friend, had asked if he could hold a beach party on our land at the north end of Chesterman Beach, and I had given him the okay.

I waited and waited for the locum to show up, and when it got to be 9:30, I decided to go see how the beach party was going. I told the head nurse I would be back shortly and left in my car.

When I got to Chesterman, maybe 15 people were sitting around on logs, and I was given a beer. About ten minutes later the RCMP erupted out of the bush, and Nick and I were told we would be charged with drinking beer in a public place. I learned later that the RCMP had had their differences with Nick and this was payback. I was in the wrong place at the wrong time.

In the meantime, I was free to go, so my family and I went on our camping trip, up to Williams Lake and back through the Okanagan. When we were in Kelowna, the morning paper announced that the premier had dropped the writ on July 21. Election day was August 27.

Back home in Tofino, I jumped right into electioneering. I had the same team, Ron Burley and Jack Walter, we ran a good campaign, and we won by a good majority, though it was slightly smaller than my first time. Social Credit once again formed the government of the province, and W.A.C. Bennett returned as premier.

Campaigning in Port Alberni with W.A.C. Bennett, Lynn, and Dan Campbell (in the front seat).

Pacific Rim Park

Now that the election was over, I had to turn my attention to the serious charge of drinking in a public place. I was not certain what the exact charge was or what the consequences might be if I were convicted. Would I have to give up my seat? I did not know. I did know that I would have to hire legal counsel, but that was expensive, and I didn't know how much time or money it would take or who I could hire.

These last questions were answered one evening in the fall of 1969 when I received a phone call. The voice at the other end said, "We see from the newspaper that you are in a bit of legal trouble."

"Yes," I said.

"Could you use a little help?"

"It would depend on the cost," says I.

"The cost will be naught."

"Feel free to come," I replied.

It was my old friend and neighbour from Prince Albert, Clyne Harradence, offering his and his brother Milt's services pro bono. Milt, former head of the Conservative Party of Alberta, was the best-known criminal lawyer in Alberta, and Clyne, an associate of John Diefenbaker, was the best-known criminal lawyer in Saskatchewan. What a wonderful surprise. What a coup!

I was talking the next day to the corporal of the Tofino RCMP detachment, who had recently transferred from Calgary. He asked who would be defending me when the charges came to trial, and I said, "Milt Harradence." An indescribable look came over his face as he exclaimed, "Oh shit."

Both lawyers had to get dispensation from the BC Law Society to argue a case in British Columbia. But as they were doing it pro bono, there was no problem. They flew in to the Vancouver airport and were met there by Herb Capozzi, my friend and seatmate in the legislature. Herb's family owned Calona Wines and had a company plane, which flew the three of them to the Tofino airport. Herb, a tall, good-looking man of Italian descent, happened to be wearing cowboy boots and a cowboy hat, and Milt described him as being a cross between Hoss Cartwright and Rudolph Valentino.

We spent the night before the trial at my house, lining up our defence strategy, and the next day we arrived at the office in the small Tofino firehall and RCMP station that served as a courtroom. The presiding judge was Eric Winch, who at one time had been a Liberal candidate in Nanaimo.

The trial got underway with the prosecutor asking me, "Were you on the beach on this night?"

"Yes," I replied.

"And you were sitting on a log?"

"Yes."

"Were you holding and drinking from a beer bottle?"

"Yes."

"And was there alcohol in the beer?"

"I would surely hope so," I said.

"Did you hand the bottle to the constable?"

"Yes."

The prosecutor then entered the bottle into evidence. Clyne immediately asked if this was the bottle and if the constable had signed his initials.

"Yes," he said.

"Show us your initials," said Clyne.

The constable was so rattled he couldn't point them out. He said that there were other bottles in a case in their office next door, and he assumed that my bottle was in that case; could he leave to look for it?

Clyne immediately said, "Your Honour, please advise this witness that he not talk to anyone while away from this courtroom."

He was so advised. The constable left the courtroom for the RCMP office, opened the door and immediately blurted out to the corporal, "Where's the fucking bottle?"

Unbeknownst to him, Clyne had quietly tiptoed out behind him and heard the exchange. Clyne returned and told the court what had happened. The judge, in high dudgeon, warned the constable "that even the RCMP could be held in contempt of this court."

My lawyers asked that the charge be thrown out as the RCMP couldn't produce the evidence. This request was denied, and the trial continued, but it soon wrapped up. The result, as reported in the *Vancouver Sun* of October 6, 1969: "Dismissing the case, provincial court judge Eric Winch agreed that the party had been on private property but said the point at issue was whether the liquor consumption had 'drawn the attention of the public.' He concluded: 'There were complaints, but there is no evidence that this (party) was a wild, rangitang affair. I cannot say that the attention of the public was drawn. I discharge the accused.'"

When I worked summers at the Banff Springs Hotel while I was attending medical school, I made friends with students from across the country. After this judgment hit the press, I got calls from many of them, the gist of which was, "We never knew you to be at a party that wasn't a rangitang affair, McDiarmid."

Luckily, none of this had proved detrimental to my re-election in Port Alberni. I was, after all, the drinking man's friend.

Twelve

McDiarmid's Farewell

At every opportunity, during the 1969 election campaign, my Liberal opponent had accused me of neglecting my constituents, claiming, "The only people who see McDiarmid are his patients."

There was only a grain of truth to this, as people who had problems they wanted their MLA to deal with were quick to phone or write a letter if they wanted action. However, I realized that I would have to deal with my isolation from Port Alberni if I wanted to continue in politics.

During most of this time I was the sole doctor in Tofino, on call night and day, day in and day out, except for two months when the legislature was in session. For those months I had to secure the services of a locum.

The hospital was well run, and we were fortunate to have not only a good matron and nursing staff, but also excellent support staff in the laundry, under Katie Monks. We were quick to institute isolation procedures at any hint of infection, and as a result we had a low incidence of post-surgical wound infection. I was able to persuade a range of surgical specialists to come to Tofino and do procedures so patients could stay at home near relatives and loved ones, considerably reducing costs.

I had taken some surgical training in England in 1959, so I was able to do a substantial number of elective procedures such as tonsillectomies, hernias, varicose veins, hysterectomies and low-segment caesarean sections, and I continued to deliver over 100 babies every year. In all my time in Tofino, we had no maternity fatalities. The fact that we could do emergency caesarean sections had a lot to do with this. I set numerous fractures. The oldest patient I ever operated on was an 85-year-old miner/prospector who scoffed at my suggestion that he was too old for hernia surgery and should consider a truss. I told him he could go back to work in six weeks, but he was back in three.

In all my time in Tofino, we had only one death that resulted from a surgical procedure. A young woman from Ahousat was admitted with abdominal bleeding from a ruptured ectopic pregnancy in a Fallopian tube. I had removed the ectopic and was closing the abdominal wound when a massive clot broke loose from either her pelvis or her legs and lodged in her lungs. The doctor administering the anesthetic was unable to revive her. This is not something that can be prevented. I saw the same thing happen to a healthy 21-year-old during a cast removal at Vancouver General.

I think it was early 1969 when a slow burnout started, caused by a combination of being on call continuously and being unable to attract a second doctor due to the low rate the federal government paid for our work with the local Natives. The feds said they were not responsible for funding Native health care, even though they had hospitals devoted to Native patients and employed Indian Health nurses. Independent physicians like me were paid 25 cents on the dollar, and if, at this munificent rate of pay, you billed over $300 in a month, that was the cap. This was not too onerous when a clinic of five or six doctors shared the burden, but it was disastrous for solo practitioners in remote areas with many Native patients—a perfect description of Tofino.

When it seemed like things couldn't get any worse, the hospital board received a letter from some bureaucrat in Victoria questioning why the board allowed elective surgery in such a small facility. If the bureaucrat were able to eliminate surgery, he would take away the part of the practice I was best at and got the most satisfaction from. It would also greatly diminish the hospital's value to the community. I expected strong support from the hospital board, but when I approached Tom Gibson his reply was "We will send a letter." I was surprised that the board would not defend the hospital more vigorously, but I could see the writing was on the wall and it was time to make plans to leave.

It took six long months to sell our house, and then the residents of Tofino and Ucluelet threw a dance and farewell party at a large hall at the airport. We received many gifts and testimonials, but my most prized possession to this day is a composition by Harry Taylor of Ucluelet. Harry and I were not political allies, but we were curling buddies, and I had looked after Harry, his wife, their kids and his elderly parents for many years.

McDiarmid's Farewell

The Accused now stands before us, and the judge has heard his case
How he carried on and capered, and debased the human race.
You have curled in your pyjamas, got the jeep stuck on the road
Wrecked the boat at Migeon River and damn near lost your load.

You really stole a big piano, while on a wild spree
Got people drunk on Grey Cup Day as you passed the booze out free.
You were even charged with drinking in a public place
Drove up and down the highway as if you were in a race.

You've carried on and capered and led a pretty hectic life
But what we cannot understand is how you got such a real nice wife.
But she's not blameless either and may be a little bit insane

For she flew over the Rockies with you in an itty bitty plane.
Her dog attacked the mover as he carried out his chores
I'm sure she must be guilty cause Tigger should have been outdoors.

You only had Sea Bee, twas the best you could afford just yet
So you ran for Social Credit so you could get a big lear jet
And be like Phil Gaglardi and fly it all around
It would really be a promotion for an ex-councillor from Tofino town.

You and Col. MacGuggin are going before the liquor board I hear
To discuss the virtues of Ben Ginter's cans of beer
I feel your friend Capozzi will think you quite a swine
Because he thinks you only drink his Dad's Calona wine
So I'm afraid that you will be the loser in the end
Even though you're known as the drinking man's best friend.

Now Howie and Lynn are leaving and it is a crying shame
But you who voted Socred have only yourselves to blame
Now we know that when you leave here, the place will never be the same
But I'm not sure that our loss will be Port Alberni's Gain
For they're not as tough as we are and I'm sure that they will yell
And tell old wacky Bennett every time that you raise Hell.

Now you stand for judgment by the people in this room
And even though you know them well I forecast your doom
Now we all here think it so I'll say it to your face
Howie, as a doctor you will never be replaced.

Now that you and Lynn are leaving we wish you all the best
We hope that Port Alberni gives you loads of happiness
And in your new venture we hope you do real great
And make lots of money selling Real Estate.

Harry Taylor
Ucluelet, BC
November 28, 1969

We rented a modest house on 3rd Avenue in Port Alberni, right near the pulp mill. I jerry-rigged a small office in the basement and was open for business, and the boys enrolled in various public schools.

We all enjoyed living in Port, but Lynn still found it difficult raising three boys while I was away in the legislature. Politics was just not her bag. The Social Credit ladies adored her and asked me to ask her if she would pour tea at a fundraiser they were putting on. I asked, and after a minute she gave me a direct look and said, "You're the politician. You go to the tea party!!"

Port Alberni was a great sports town, and we all enjoyed the big indoor pool at Echo Centre. Lynn and I both curled. I established a good working relationship with Mayor Fred Bishop and his administrator Jim Sawyer, who I had come to know during the amalgamation of Alberni and Port Alberni. I had a particularly good relationship with the Ministry of Municipal Affairs, under the direction of my friend Dan Campbell, and could be an effective intermediary between the city and the ministry. Mayor Bishop paid me my most prized accolade as a politician. He said, "We may not always agree with you, McDiarmid, but we always know where you stand."

Thirteen

The Park Becomes a Reality

With the election of 1969 behind us, the first session of the new legislature began in January 1970. It was over nine months since the enabling legislation for the park was passed, and I was becoming frustrated by the lack of official reports on its progress. I was able to glean some information that I believed was accurate. It suggested that there was a consensus about the Long Beach and Effingham Islands sections but extreme controversy over including the life-saving trail, and this controversy threatened the park's existence.

On January 20, 1970, I made a speech in the legislature urging both sides to compromise and at least proclaim those lands about which there was agreement. I was concerned about the escalating costs of property in the area.

Finally, on April 21, 1970, Ken Kiernan and Jean Chrétien signed an agreement creating a national park on the west coast of Vancouver Island. The agreement was ratified by the provincial cabinet as the West Coast National Park Act on April 27, 1970, and was signed into law when it received royal assent from Lieutenant Governor J.R. Nicholson the next day, April 28, 1970. It was a great day!

The main result of the agreement was that Part I lands (Clayoquot) and Part II lands (Barclay), more familiarly known as Long Beach and Effingham Islands, were surveyed, their boundaries were given precise legal description for the first time (it turned out my Chesterman Beach property was not included), and they were designated park lands. Part III lands (Renfrew), better known as the life-saving trail or the West Coast Trail, were subject to a ground survey. This effectively postponed the decision on how much land would eventually make up the West Coast Trail. Section 7 of the agreement reaffirmed that British Columbia and Canada would share acquisition costs equally.

There were two sections of particular interest to me. The first stated: "Canada and British Columbia will take such measures as may be necessary to extinguish the interest of Indians in any of the lands within the proposed National Park."

The reason Parks Canada gave me for not granting life tenancy to some landholders was that it couldn't allow this when even Indian reserves were to be extinguished. However, the Natives turned out to be less compliant about turning over their land and took full advantage of their political clout to maintain the right to their lands. In contrast, the privately held homes on south Long Beach were bought and destroyed, with the exception of one house that is still used by Parks Canada as an office.

The second paragraph of interest to me was the one that said: "Now therefore this agreement witnesses that in consideration of the promises and the agreements herein contained, subject always to the appropriation of funds therefor by the Parliament of Canada and the Legislature of British Columbia." Trust a politician to always create a way out.

I was not really worried about the province coming up with its share of the money as long as I had the backing of the "old man," and I was sure I did. "You will get your park," he had said. I was confident it was a done deal.

And, indeed, in 1971, the centennial of British Columbia's entry into the Canadian confederation, there was a dedication ceremony for the Long Beach section of the park. It marked the turnover of provincial land to the Government of Canada. I was included in the official party, but the prominent figures were ministers Kiernan and Chrétien. The formal dedication took place on Long Beach on May 4, 1971, with Princess Anne presiding.

Dedication of Long Beach section of Pacific Rim National Park by Princess Anne, May 4, 1971. Ken Kiernan is at the lectern; Princess Anne is behind him, and Jean Chrétien is to her right. I am at far left, wearing a Nuu-chah-nulth cedar bark hat.

By this time, many properties had been expropriated, and it seemed likely the October 1, 1972, deadline for such acquisitions would be met. Not all my constituents were happy about this because they were losing their land or their homes. The controversy over the West Coast Trail continued and ultimately escalated as the Sierra Club and other groups lobbied for the inclusion of a heavily forested area known as the Nitinat Triangle. This was opposed by the forest industry, and Ray Williston, the provincial minister of Lands and Forests, became actively involved. The dispute continued even after I left the legislature.

In March 1972 I fought one last battle for the park when Kiernan, exasperated by the controversy over the Nitinat Triangle, said that British Columbia would trade two lakes in the Triangle for Long Beach. I opposed this as strongly as I could, and it did not happen.

In 1973, the West Coast Trail section was officially added to the park and opened for hikers. But my dream had been realized in 1971 when the Long Beach section was dedicated.

Fourteen

Tahsis and Other Events

I had other matters to deal with besides the park. The community of Tahsis, in the northernmost part of my constituency, was a logging company town of 1,500 to 2,000 people. The company owned all the homes and provided all the services to the townsite and the sawmill, which provided the jobs. The only access was by boat or by seaplane. Over time, dissatisfaction with this state of affairs gradually increased. Residents wanted more freedom, particularly to own their own homes, and the company was sick of the headaches involved in allocating homes as well as having to pay the rising costs of electricity and infrastructure maintenance.

The government's policy at that time was to encourage company towns to become municipalities, and the Ministry of Municipal Affairs was prepared to offer significant incentives to see this happen. Various ministries were involved in the process of improving road access and supplying hydro to these communities, and these ministries often worked in isolation and ended up proposing solutions that conflicted with the ideas of other ministries. Ray Williston, minister of Lands and Forests, asked me to establish and chair an informal committee of all interested parties so the effort in Tahsis would be coordinated.

The committee developed a plan to build a road from Tahsis to Gold River and establish the hydro line alongside the road, which would allow much easier hydro maintenance than a previously proposed route. The road would also provide greater access to timberlands along the way.

With all this decided, on July 15, 1970, I was able to present letters patent to a new municipality on what I described as its birthday. During the ceremony I told Tahsis residents that I had ordered a large bouquet from a florist in Campbell River but was horrified to find out that morning that they had erroneously sent a funeral bouquet. When I phoned to complain, the florist said, "You think you've got problems. Somewhere in a cemetery in Campbell River is a large bouquet with the inscription 'Lots of luck under the new administration.'"

≕≡

I was sitting in the legislature on February 19, 1970, when the Deputy Speaker recognized "the Honourable Second Member for Vancouver South." Agnes Kripps rose to speak.

We were in the midst of the debate on the budget, and she began benignly enough, talking about inflation and education, moving on to talk about the family and its unique place in society (and I quote here directly from Hansard): "We must direct our efforts in such a way that the family continues in the future to hold its unique place in society with its human values and ideals. It is for this reason, Mr. Speaker, that I believe sex education should be taught in our schools as a supplement to what our children receive in the home. Unfortunately, our sex education programme is inadequate. I would therefore suggest, Mr. Speaker, since 1970 is international education year, that our Minister of Education takes a bold step forward and initiates action for a sex education programme in our schools."

The problem, according to Agnes, was "not related to the problem of the education or the teaching part of the programme but rather to the word itself—that nasty little three-letter word, Sex, which carries with it a stigma and a distorted connotation." She went on to give several definitions of sex and said:

> Because so many shades of meaning have been written into the word, I have come to hate it, and I propose [laughter] I hate the word sex, and I propose that we throw it out of the vocabulary of education—let's find a substitute and start all over again.
>
> SOME HON MEMBERS: NO! NO!
>
> MRS. KRIPPS: ...Let's standardize the word so that it means the same to everybody. Let's call it...Listen carefully now, let's call it, for example, BOLT. That stands for B for Biology of Life Today...That's just an example. [laughter]...You may have other words you would like to use [applause and laughter]...Let's call it the word Bolt. Then we can tackle the problem afresh so that when we talk about bolt education in schools we're not going to become involved in moral or religious aspects of its meaning. We will face bolt education with a fresh, open mind...By eliminating the word sex and replacing it with Bolt or any other word...we will remove the blindfolds, the smirks, the embarrassment and, above all, the ignorance.
>
> AN HON. MEMBER: Call it Social Credit (laughter)

It is not in Hansard, but I saw Bob Strachan rise from his seat and say, "I'm going to Bolt out of here."

Herb Capozzi, who spoke after Agnes, welcomed us to a "bolt new world" and said that, "if nothing else, she had everyone bolt upright in their chairs," adding, "There is a little poem that says, 'It makes me wonder, Mr. Member – And indeed it takes much telling – Why a word that's so much fun – Is so dirty in the spelling.'"

The House is usually such a boring place, even a small bit of levity is much appreciated.

On a later date, Agnes came to my rescue when we were assembled for our regular caucus meeting. W.A.C. rarely attended caucus, so one of the senior cabinet ministers would take the chair. On this day, Les Peterson, a very accomplished minister, handled the meeting with aplomb. Always well coiffed and immaculately dressed, he was not easily rattled.

He told us that the government had received a request from the plastic and reconstructive surgery branch of the BC Medical Association to lower the age of consent for surgery. There had been a number of recent cases of minors with disfiguring conditions who were unable to obtain parental consent to remedy those conditions, and the doctors found this troubling.

The meeting was thrown open for discussion. As a medical doctor, I was strongly in favour of lowering the age of consent, but I reserved my opinion until late in the debate. However, when the member representing North Okanagan—a staunch Catholic who strongly opposed the proposal because it would also lower the age of consent for abortion—went on to say that the existing law was a strong deterrent to boys making advances to girls in the back seats of cars, forcing them to think twice about going any further, I couldn't refrain from responding.

Spontaneously and imprudently I said, "Mr. Chairman, has the member from North Okanagan never heard that a hard cock has no conscience?"

There was sudden silence. Les Peterson looked apoplectic. I thought the buttons would fly off his vest. Herb Capozzi looked at me as if I were a condemned man.

Finally, after an eternity of silence, Agnes Kripps blurted, "This is some cockus."

She broke the tension, everyone laughed and I was saved from certain exile.

Fifteen

Oak Bay

By early 1972, the Alberni constituency was in good shape. Passing lanes were open on the road from Port Alberni to the east coast. The relocation of Highway 4 was almost complete, as was the acquisition of land for the park.

Since it was three years since the 1969 election, we knew it was almost inevitable that the "old man" would go to the polls this year, but I was getting tired of being away from my family when the House was sitting, and Lynn was finding it a challenge raising three boys alone. I wanted to continue in politics if I could, and it occurred to me that this might be possible if we moved to Victoria and I was able to win a seat there. My friend Tom Johnstone agreed to seek the Socred nomination in Alberni, and I knew that if he were elected, the riding would be in good hands.

It so happened that the Oak Bay constituency had an opening for a Social Credit candidate because Dr. Scott Wallace, who had won Oak Bay in 1969 as a Socred, had become disenchanted with our party and crossed the floor to represent the Conservatives. Lynn and I found a house on Ten Mile Point, which was in the constituency, and I set out to win the nomination.

I was not a natural fit. I had too many rough edges for wealthy, sophisticated Oak Bay, which had been the graveyard of many Socred candidates. Scott Wallace was very much the exception, and the feeling was that he had won it on his own, as a maverick, rather than as a result of his party affiliation. Grace McCarthy was a great help to me in securing the nomination, but W.A.C. was not happy at all. He knew instinctively that Alberni was a much better fit for me than Oak Bay. He even suggested there was the possibility of a cabinet post if I stayed put. I couldn't.

I won the nomination, and Ron Burley came down to be my campaign manager. It soon became apparent that I was a square peg in a round hole. I related a whole lot better to loggers, millworkers and fishermen than I did to doctors, lawyers and accountants. I had one debate with Scott Wallace, and I performed badly.

When the election was over, I had been thrashed in Oak Bay, and my friend Tom Johnstone had been beaten in Alberni. As a result, a new NDP member got to cut the ribbon on Highway 4 after all my work. Actually, a lot of Socred candidates got thrashed. From a 38-seat majority in 1969, Social Credit dropped to 10 seats in 1972. The NDP were victorious. I can attest to the fact that post-election parties are a lot more fun when you have won.

Now I had to find a job, and quickly. One day when I was doing surgical assists, I met Carl Whiteside, who had a practice in Brentwood Bay. It was a 30-minute drive from our home on Ten Mile Point, which meant sleeping on the office floor those nights I was on call, but it was a badly needed job. Carl and I hit it off personally. He was an astute physician, and we soon became partners. The property taxes on our landholdings in Tofino were increasing rapidly each year, and the cash flow I had as a practising physician was a great improvement over the salary of a backbench MLA.

Sixteen

The Cabin

Shell Beach lies between Chesterman and McKenzie beaches south of Tofino. In the 1950s, the only access was over a rough trail from the north end of Chesterman. Shell Beach is small, only 300 feet long, but it faces south and is well protected from the cold westerly winds that blow hard in the summer when the sun shines.

Lynn and I came frequently to a small rocky promontory at the north end of Shell. We would unfold a red-and-white tablecloth and enjoy wine and cheese. I would point to the rocks just in front of the tree line and say, "This is where the cabin will go." The only problem was that George Pownall still owned the land.

Many years later, along about 1977, we finally acquired the land. We were living in Victoria but decided that we should have a physical presence in Tofino, preferably on the rocky promontory at the north end of Shell Beach. We needed to know if a building there would be safe from high waves during a big winter storm. One November afternoon I embarked on a flight with my friend Gary Richards, who owned Tofino Air and was a superb pilot. The wind from a fierce storm had just abated, but the tide was high and the swells gigantic.

As we flew over the beach, we could see that our proposed building site was safely out of the water, but the sea flowed in behind it, making the promontory an island for an hour or two during the highest of the tides. This was where the cabin could and would go.

I started to design a small cabin, a post-and-beam affair so as to allow large windows that would take advantage of a 270-degree view of the ocean. I had at least three builders look at the site, but they all said it was a logistical nightmare. No road, no water, no electricity. None of them would even attempt to build there. Gary Gibson suggested I talk with Don McGinnis, who had just recently moved to Tofino. He looked at the site and said, "No problem!"

Don hired an assistant, Henry Nolla, who was an expert at adzing wood; together they produced a generator and a winch, and constructed a tramline from the site down to the beach. Building materials were loaded onto a herring skiff in Tofino and brought ashore at high tide, then winched up the tramline to the site. Henry was frequently the skipper on the herring skiff, which was hard to manoeuvre because the entrance to Shell Beach is ringed with low rocks, necessitating deliveries at high tide and sometimes at night. On at least two occasions, the skiff overturned.

When the cabin was finished, it was compact, consisting of a bathroom, kitchen and all-purpose front room that served as living room, dining room and bedrooms. The main bearing rafter was cut from a cedar on the property using an Alaska mill. It was 6 inches wide, 14 inches deep, 46 feet long and went at a 30-degree slope. The front bearing post went through the fireplace and out the other side over a large deck.

The cabin was still only accessible by trail from Chesterman Beach, but Don was concerned about potential vandalism, something I hadn't thought about. Don said that Henry could, in short order, "throw up" a place at the head of the trail and become custodian and protector of the cabin. Thus began a friendship that was just a joy for 25 years.

The fireplace at our cabin on Shell Beach. After a fire destroyed the cabin in the late 1980s, this was the only thing left standing.

The second incarnation of the Shell Beach cabin under construction.

There are enough cabin stories to fill a book of their own, of which two involve Dick Samson, my next-door neighbour in Victoria, and his son Paul. Paul was about eight at the time. It was getting dusk and we were doing the dishes.

Paul was interested in the big glass floats we had scattered around the front room. We proceeded to tell him they were from Japanese fishing nets and had broken off and floated across the Pacific. He thought we were pulling his leg and didn't believe us at all.

Suddenly, in front of the big picture window above the sink, a young, unmistakably Japanese woman appeared.

Dick and I, in unison, said, "There, Paul! Another one has just washed up!"

It turned out she was a stewardess from Japan Airlines who was exploring around the rocks with her boyfriend and had gotten lost.

On another visit, Dick, Paul, my eldest son Charles and I decided to treat ourselves to a bacon-and-egg breakfast at the venerable Maquinna Hotel. We all ordered, and I asked for my bacon crisp. Three of the orders arrived and were almost finished before mine arrived with limp bacon. I pointed this out to the server and asked him to take it back, which he did, only to return seconds later, the bacon unchanged, with the admonition, "Cook says, 'That's as crisp as I can get it.'"

From then on, in both families, when something didn't go just right or success eluded you, "That's as crisp as I can get it" said it all.

When we acquired the rocky promontory where the cabin eventually appeared, we also bought the site at the north end of Chesterman where I wanted the hotel to go. This was where I had told myself "one day" when I first saw it.

During the early negotiations between the province and the federal government, I made a strong case for the Wickaninnish Inn on the south end of Long Beach to remain in

Lynn and I with Henry Nolla (right), a valued friend who helped build our cabin and who became its custodian and protector for many years after.

operation. The inn had been granted a five-year lease when Pacific Rim National Park was established, but there was an uneasy relationship between the inn and Parks Canada. Robin Fells, who had managed the property in an exemplary fashion, had left, and it ceased to be well-managed. Five years later, it was clear that Parks Canada didn't want a private company operating in a national park and would not renew the lease. Nonetheless, when the official announcement was made, there was a storm of protest from across Canada over the impending closure. The inn had truly become an icon. Among the most prominent objectors was Grace McCarthy, minister of Recreation and Travel Industry in Bill Bennett's Socred cabinet, elected in 1975. She wrote to the federal minister stating, in part, "It is imperative that a lodging be retained within Pacific Rim National Park."

It was all to no avail, and I felt a great deal of guilt. If I hadn't promoted the park, the Wick would still be operating.

Paul (left) and Dick Samson at the Shell Beach cabin

The entrance doors at Wickaninnish Inn – hand carved by Henry Nolla.

The site we had on Chesterman closely approximated the Wicka-ninnish Inn site, and I made up my mind to try to re-create the Wick on Chesterman.

My Victoria friend Dick Samson was a lawyer. He did some sleuth-ing and found out that when the feds expropriated the Wick, they purchased only the building, not the company, Wickaninnish Inn Ltd. As the inn was the company's only asset, they saw no reason to pay annual fees to keep the company in good standing, and after three years of delinquency, the name could be purchased by anyone who applied for it. Dick discovered the date it would become available, and on that morning I was at the wicket of the registrar of companies even before the office opened.

I shake hands with Jean Chrétien under the porte cochère of the new Wick Inn. To Chrétien's left is Charles McDiarmid, owner-manager of the Inn, and beside him is Ike Seaman, long-time Wick employee.

We now had the site and the name for my dream hotel. We also had very valuable land assets but minimal cash, so we set about attempting to interest outside investors in the project while I continued to practise medicine with Carl Whiteside. We approached many private investors and every financial institution known to man, to no avail. All thought it was far too risky a project.

During this time, the value of the land was increasing rapidly. That was the good news. The bad news was that the property taxes increased in lockstep. I needed to find more income to preserve the site. The answer was to earn my licence to practise in the United States, where doctors were not only paid more but were paid in US dollars, which at that time were worth Can$1.40. We lived in California for ten years, continually trying to secure investors, without any luck. Eventually I decided that if the inn was ever to be built, we would need to return to Canada to work on-site.

I must admit, there were times I wondered if this was all worthwhile when we could simply sell the land and be financially secure, but my family had come to share my vision and held firm. After many years we finally attracted enough investors, many of whom were Tofino residents who had great faith in the area, and on August 9, 1996, the new Wick Inn opened for business almost 20 years after we acquired the name.

How this all came to pass is a fascinating story in its own right, which I hope to tell on another day, but for now, *That's as crisp as I can get it.*

Postscript

Wickaninnish—A Wondrous Place

The inn is quiet. There is the warmth of the fireplace adding both comfort and charming coziness to the room. Somewhere in this building there is laughter and much discussion going on. The culinary staff is preparing a memorable dining experience.

But right now, for us, in this Wickaninnish retreat, our room overlooks an ever-changing sea. Sometimes it's turbulent, raging up against the shore with the force of a gale. Later the waves will lap at the shore and remind us that the storm is over. We are calm again and absorbing the quiet and beauty of nature.

We realize how fortunate we are. What a treasure we have discovered.

It's an unforgettable space—and an unforgettable state of mind.

It's Wickaninnish Inn.

And it's saved for all time.

Howie McDiarmid's tenacity has carried him through some financially troubled waters as, over many years, he established the new Wickaninnish Inn to become the world-class resort of today. As acclaim for the inn builds (for example, *Travel & Leisure* magazine subscribers named it the #1 hotel in North America and #3 in the world in 2002), Howie and the McDiarmid family are still at the helm, welcoming visitors from near and far who come to rejuvenate their spirits, experience dramatic Pacific storms, walk a breathtaking beach for miles, watch the whales, and return to be embraced by the hospitality of the unequalled Wickaninnish Inn.

Grace McCarthy, OC, OBC

Vancouver, April 2009